# Fodor's POCKET

# dublin

**fifth edition**

D0366014

Excerpted from Fodor's Ireland

fodor's travel publications
new york • toronto • london • sydney • auckland
www.fodors.com

# contents

on the road with fodor's                        iv

Don't Forget to Write  v

📖 introducing dublin                            2

🪧 here and there                               14

🍴 eating out                                   78

🛍 shopping                                      98

☼ outdoor activities and sports               112

🍸 nightlife and the arts                      120

🏢 where to stay                               140

💡 practical information                       160

📄 index                                       195

## maps

dublin city center 20–21

dublin west 48–49

dublin dining 84–85

dublin shopping 101

dublin pubs 133

dublin lodging 152–153

# on the road with fodor's

**A TRIP TAKES YOU OUT OF YOURSELF.** Concerns of life at home disappear, driven away by more immediate thoughts—about, say, what marvels will beguile the next day, or where you'll have dinner. That's where Fodor's comes in. We make sure that you know all your options in Dublin, so that you don't miss something that's around the next bend just because you didn't know it was there. Mindful that the best memories of your trip might have nothing to do with what you came to to see, we guide you to sights large and small. With Fodor's at your side, serendipitous discoveries are never far away.

Our success in showing you every corner of Dublin is a credit to our extraordinary writers. They're the kind of people you'd poll for travel advice if you knew them.

**Graham Bolger** is a freelance writer who contributes to a wide variety of titles in Ireland, specializing in travel, music, and technical writing. He is currently working on a series of self-help books. A consummate fan of all things edible, he updated the Eating Out chapter.

**Anto Howard** is a Northside Dublin native who studied at Trinity College before acquiring his U.S. green card. He lived in New York, where he worked as a travel writer, editor, and playwright, before returning to Ireland. Anto (short for Anthony) is also the author of *Fodor's Escape to Ireland*.

You can rest assured that you're in good hands—and that no property mentioned in the book has paid to be included. Each has been selected strictly on its merits, as the best of its type in its price range.

## Don't Forget to Write

Your experiences—positive and negative—matter to us. If we have missed or misstated something, we want to hear about it. We follow up on all suggestions. Contact the Dublin editors at editors@fodors.com or c/o Fodor's at 1745 Broadway, New York, NY 10019. And have a fabulous trip!

*Karen Cure*

Karen Cure
*Editorial Director*

# dublin

## In This Chapter

PLEASURES AND PASTIMES 8 · Literary Dublin 8 · Musical Dublin 8 · A Thousand Pubs 9 · QUICK TOURS 10 · If You Have One Day 10 · If You Have Three Days 12 · If You Have Five Days 13

# introducing dublin

**IN HIS INIMITABLE,** irresistible way, James Joyce immortalized Dublin in his *Ulysses*, *Dubliners*, and *A Portrait of the Artist as a Young Man*, filling his works with the people he knew, with their own words, and with not a few of his own. As it turns out, he became one of Dublin's most famous exiles. Disappointed with the city's provincial outlook and small-town manners, he departed in 1902, at the age of 20 (his famed peers Sean O'Casey and Samuel Beckett soon followed). If, however, Joyce was to return to his genteel hometown today and take an extended, quasi-Homeric odyssey through the city (as he does so famously in *Ulysses*), would he even recognize Dublin as his "Dear Dirty Dumpling, foostherfather of fingalls and dotthergills"?

What would he make of Temple Bar—the city's erstwhile down-at-heels neighborhood now crammed with restaurants and stylish hotels in its reborn state as Dublin's "Left Bank"? Or the old market area of Smithfield, whose makeover has seen it transformed into an impressive plaza and summer venue for big-name concerts? Or of the new Irishness, where every aspect of Celtic culture is red-hot: from Frank McCourt's *Angela's Ashes*, which dominated best-seller lists in the United States (the movie version was shot in the city and elsewhere around the country), to *Riverdance*, the old Irish mass-jig gone global? Plus, the returned Joyce would be stirred by the songs of U2, fired up by the films of Neil Jordan, and moved by the poems of Nobel laureate Seamus Heaney. In short, Irish is way in. As for Ireland's capital, elegant shops and hotels, galleries, art-house cinemas, coffeehouses, and a stunning variety of restaurants are springing up on almost every street in Dublin, transforming the genteel capital that once suffocated Joyce into a city almost as cosmopolitan as the Paris to which he fled.

Forget the Vikings and the English. Fast-forward to the new Dublin, where the army of invaders landing at the intersection of O'Connell Street and Temple Lane are London lads on a wild bachelor night, Europeans in search of a chic weekend getaway, and representatives from the United States of the "FBI"—or foreign-born Irish. Thanks to "the Celtic Tiger"—the nickname given to the roaring Irish economy—this most intimate capital city in Western Europe has become a boomtown.

Happily, enough of the old Dublin remains to enchant. After all, it's the fundamentals—the Georgian elegance of Merrion Square, the Norman drama of Christ Church Cathedral, a foamy pint at an atmospheric pub—that still gratify. Fittingly, some of the more recent developments hark back to the earliest. Two multimedia shows in the downtown area remind us that Norsemen (various neighborhood names, such as Howth, Leixlip, and Dalkey, echo their historic presence) were responsible for the city's original boom. In ancient days, more than 1,500 years ago, Dublin had been little more than a crossroads—albeit a critical one—of four of the main thoroughfares that traversed the country. Then, it had two names: Baile Atha Cliath, meaning City of the Hurdles, which was bestowed by Celtic traders in the 2nd century AD and which you can still see on buses and billboards throughout the city, and Dubhlinn, or "dark pool" (the murkiness of the water was caused by peat), which is believed to have been where Dublin Castle now stands.

In 837, Norsemen from Scandinavia carried out the first invasion on Dublin, only to be followed by other waves of warriors staking their claim to the city—from the 12th-century Anglo-Normans to Oliver Cromwell in 1651. Not until the 18th century did Dublin reach a period of glory, when a golden age of enlightened patronage by wealthy nobles turned the city into one of Europe's most prepossessing capitals. Streets and squares, such as Merrion and Fitzwilliam squares, were constructed with neoclassic dignity and Palladian grace. If, today, Dublin is still redolent in parts of the elegance of the 18th century, it is due to the eminently refined Georgian style of art and architecture, which flowered in the city between 1714 and 1820 during the English reigns of the three Georges. To satisfy the taste for luxury of the often-titled, unusually wealthy members of society, lemon-color chintz borders, gilded Derbyshire pier tables, and Adamesque wood paneling were installed in the salons of town houses. The arts also flourished: Handel, the German-born English composer, wrote much of his great oratorio *Messiah* here, where it was first performed in 1742. But the aura of "the glorious eighteenth" was short-lived; in 1800, the Act of Union brought Ireland and Britain together in a common United Kingdom, and political power moved from Dublin to London. Dublin quickly lost its cultural and social sparkle as many members of the nobility moved to the new power center, turning Ireland practically overnight into "the Cinderella of all nations," in historian Maurice Craig's words.

The 19th century proved to be a time of political turmoil and agitation, although Daniel O'Connell, the first Catholic lord mayor of Dublin (his statue dominates O'Connell Street), won early success with the introduction of Catholic emancipation in 1829. During the late 1840s, Dublin escaped the worst effects of the famine, caused by potato blight, that ravaged much of southern and western Ireland. As an emerging Victorian middle class introduced an element of genteel snobbery to the city, Dublin began a rapid outward expansion to the new suburban enclaves of Ballsbridge, Rathgar, and Rathmines on the southside and Clontarf and Drumcondra on the northside.

The city entered a period of cultural ferment in the first decade of the 20th century—an era that had its political apotheosis in the Easter Uprising of 1916. A war aimed at winning independence from Britain began in County Tipperary in 1919 and lasted for three years. During the Civil War, which followed the setting up of the Irish Free State in December 1921, the Four Courts and the Custom House both came under fire and were severely damaged. The capital had to be rebuilt during the 1920s. After the Civil War was over, Dublin entered a new era of political and cultural conservatism, which continued until the late 1970s. Amazingly, the major turning point in Dublin's fortunes occurred in 1972, when Ireland, emerging from 40 years of isolationism, joined the European Economic Community. In the 1980s, while the economy remained in the grasp of recession, Dublin and Ireland once again turned to the cultural sphere to announce themselves to the rest of the world. Irish musicians stormed the American and British barricades of rock-and-roll. Bob Geldof and the Boomtown Rats ("I Don't Like Mondays") and Chris de Burgh were among the most prominent of the musicians who found audiences well beyond their native shores, but it was U2 that climbed to the topmost heights of rock-and-roll stardom, that forged a permanent place in international popular culture for Irish musicians. Sinéad O'Connor, the Cranberries, and the Corrs have since followed, and more are on the fast track.

If the 1980s saw the ascent of Irish rock stars, the 1990s and the new century were truly the boom years—a decade of broadly improved economic fortunes, major capital investment, declining unemployment, and reversing patterns of immigration—all set in motion to a great extent by Ireland's participation in the EEC (now the European Union, or EU). When Ireland overwhelmingly approved the new EU treaty in 1992, it was one of the poorest European nations; it qualified for EU grants of all kinds. Since then, money has, quite simply, *poured* into Ireland—nowhere more so than in Dublin. The International Financial Services Centre, gleaming behind the two-centuries-old Custom House, is one of the most overt signs of the success the city has had in attracting leading multinational corporations, particularly those in telecommunications, software, and service industries. In 2000 the government announced that Ireland was the world's biggest exporter of software. In the spring of 1998, the Irish overwhelmingly voted in favor of membership in the single European currency; since January 2002, Ireland's main currency has been the euro and the pound has been withdrawn from circulation. The recent downturn in the global economy has slowed the Celtic Tiger to crawling pace and economists argue over the future prospects for a country so dependent on exports.

Today, roughly half of the Irish Republic's population of 3.6 million people live in Dublin and its suburbs. It's a city of young people—astonishingly so. Students from all over Ireland attend Trinity College and the city's dozen other universities and colleges. On weekends, their counterparts from Paris, London, and Rome fly in, swelling the city's youthful contingent, crowding its pubs and clubs to overflowing. After graduating, more and more young people are sticking around rather than emigrating to New York or London, filling the raft of new jobs set up by multinational corporations and contributing to the hubbub that's evident everywhere.

All this development has not been without growing pains; with London-like house prices, increased crime, and major traffic problems, Dubliners are at last suffering the woes so familiar to city dwellers around the world. An influx of immigrants has caused resentment among some of the otherwise famously hospitable Irish. "Me darlin' Dublin's dead and gone," so goes the old traditional ballad, but the rebirth, at times difficult and a little messy, has been a spectacular success.

## PLEASURES AND PASTIMES

### LITERARY DUBLIN

Dublin packs more literary punch per square foot than practically any other spot on the planet—largely because of the ferment that took hold at the end of the 19th century, when two main cultural movements emerged. In 1893, Douglas Hyde, a Protestant and later the first president of Ireland, founded the Gaelic League (Conradh na Gaelige), with a goal of preserving the Irish language and Gaelic traditions. The poet W. B. Yeats also played a pivotal role in the Irish literary renaissance. With funding from his patron Annie Horniman, Yeats and Lady Gregory founded the **Abbey Theatre** in 1903 (it opened in 1904), to develop and produce a decidedly Irish repertoire. With this new venue, and the growing prominence of such playwrights as Sean O'Casey and J. M. Synge, Irish literature thrived. The **Dublin Writers Museum** gives a terrific introduction to this story and to the more than two dozen major writers Ireland subsequently produced (at least the dead ones—living legends have to wait to be included). To go further back in literary history, head for **Trinity College,** where you can see a few pages of the legendary 9th-century *Book of Kells* and stroll through the hallowed campus where Samuel Beckett studied and where a theater now bears his name. If you're an Oscar Wilde fan, you can pay homage to him at 1 Merrion Square. The Close-Up: "ReJoyce! A Walk through James Joyce's Dublin and *Ulysses*" guides you through some key sites connected with Joyce and *Ulysses*. And if you want to stock up on anecdotes about the relationship between the pint and the pen, check out the *Dublin Literary Pub Crawl* or take a guided tour of literary pubs.

### MUSICAL DUBLIN

Music fills Dublin's streets (especially Grafton Street) and its pubs, where talk of music is as popular as the tunes themselves. Dubliners are obsessed with music of every kind and will happily discuss anything from Elvis's earliest recordings (remember Jimmy's father in *The Commitments*?) to U2's latest incarnation. The city has been the stomping ground of so many big-league rock and pop musicians that Dublin Tourism has created a "Rock 'n Stroll" Trail, which covers 16 sites, most of them in the city center and Temple Bar. It includes spots like **Bewley's Oriental Café**, where Bob Geldof and the other members of the Boomtown Rats hung out, and the Bad Ass Café, where Sinéad O'Connor once worked. You're forgiven if you think some connections between the trail sites and the musicians seem hokey, but you're not if you don't seek out Dublin's lively, present-day music scene. A number of small pubs and larger halls host live music, but the best places are midsize venues— such as the **Olympia Theatre** and the **Temple Bar Music Centre**—where you can hear well-established local acts *and* leading international artists (including world-renowned Irish musicians) playing everything from traditional and folk rock to jazz-funk and "Dubcore," a term coined to describe the city's many noisy alternative bands. Traditional Irish music (or "Trad"), very much a child of rural Ireland, is alive and kicking in the urban sprawl of Dublin. Scores of city bars are home to impromptu "sessions" and professional gigs. **The Cobblestone** in lively Smithfield is one of the most famous and atmospheric venues.

## A THOUSAND PUBS

Even if you order only a Ballygowan (the Irish Evian), a visit to an Irish pub (or two or three) is a must. The Irish public house is a national institution—down to the spectacle, at some pubs, of patrons standing at closing time to the playing of Ireland's national anthem. Samuel Beckett would often repair to one, believing a glass of Guinness stout was the best way to ward off depression. Indeed, Dublin is for the stout of heart—the city has one pub for every 450 of its 500,000 adults. There are actor's pubs, sports pubs, even pubs for "less famous literary types"

(Grogan's on South William Street). And any occasion—be it "ordinations, liquidations, cremations," as one storefront puts it—is the right occasion. Today, Irish pubs are being exported at an unprecedented rate all around the world, but in Dublin it's a different story altogether. Here, surprisingly, modern, European-style café-bars are fast replacing the capital's traditional drinking spots. The extraordinary prices being offered for the old pubs by new entrepreneurs have proven hard to resist for the longtime owners. In the city center you'll now find high-concept designer pubs with bright, arty facades and a pervasive scent of affluence. To be sure, in the City of 1,000 Pubs, you're still certain of finding a good, old-fashioned watering hole. And if you do find yourself in a new spot, surrounded by the trappings of European chic, you'll soon discover that Dubliners still enjoy good *craic*— quintessentially Irish friendly chat and lively, irony-laced conversation. Wherever you go, remember that when you order a Guinness, the barman first pours it three-quarters of the way, lets it settle, then tops it off and brings it over to the bar. You should then wait again until the top-up has settled, at which point the brew turns a deep black. The mark of a perfect pint? As you drink the glass down, the brew will leave thin rings to mark each mouthful.

## QUICK TOURS

### IF YOU HAVE ONE DAY

Touring the largest city in Ireland in the space of a single day sounds like an impossible goal, but if you're determined you can do it in the span of a single sunrise-to-sunset day. Think Dublin 101. South of the Liffey are graceful squares and fashionable terraces from Dublin's elegant Georgian heyday; interspersed with some of the city's leading sights, this area is perfect for an introductory city tour. You might begin at O'Connell Bridge— as Dublin has no central focal point, most natives have, traditionally, regarded it as the city's Piccadilly Circus or Times Square. Then head south down Westmoreland Street on your way to view one of Dublin's most spectacular buildings, James Gandon's 18th-century Parliament House, now the Bank of Ireland building. To fuel up for the walk ahead, first stop at 12 Westmoreland Street and go into Bewley's Oriental Café, an institution that has been supplying Dubliners with coffee and buns since 1842. After you drink in the grand colonnade of the Bank of Ireland building, head east to the genteel, elegant campus of Trinity College—the oldest seat of Irish learning. Your first stop should be the Library, to see the staggering Long Room and Ireland's greatest art treasure, the Book of Kells, one of the world's most famous—and most beautiful—illuminated manuscripts.

Leave the campus and take a stroll along Grafton Street, Dublin's ritziest shopping street and—"Who will buy my beautiful roses?"—open-air flower market. Appropriately enough, one of the city's favorite relaxation spots, the lovely little park of St. Stephen's Green, is nearby. Head over to the northeast corner of the park to find ground zero for the city's cultural institutions. Here, surrounding the four points of Leinster House (built by the Duke of Kildare, Ireland's first patron of Palladianism), are the National Museum, replete with artifacts and exhibits dating from prehistoric times; the National Gallery of Ireland (don't miss the Irish collection and the Caravaggio Taking of Christ); the National Library; and the Natural History Museum. Depending on your interests, pick one to explore, and then make a quick detour eastward to Merrion Square—among Dublin's most famous Georgian landmarks.

For a lovely lunch, head back to Stephen's Green and the Victorian Le Méridien Shelbourne Hotel—the lobby salons glow with Waterford chandeliers and blazing fireplaces. From Stephen's Green, hop on a bus or cab west to pay your respects to St. Paddy—St. Patrick's Cathedral. End the day exploring the cobbled streets, many cafés, and shops of Dublin's bohemian quarter, the compact Temple Bar area. Because you couldn't fit in a stop at the Guinness Brewery and Storehouse, top the evening off with a pint at the Porterhouse pub. By the time the barman says "Finish your pints" to announce closing time at 11 PM, you'll agree that although this day was a lightning tour of the city's main sights, it has left an indelible impression of what Dublin is all about.

## IF YOU HAVE THREE DAYS

The above tour is the grand curtain-raiser for this itinerary. Dedicate your second day to the north and west of the city center. In the morning, cross the Liffey via O'Connell Bridge and walk up O'Connell Street, the city's widest thoroughfare, stopping to visit the General Post Office—the besieged headquarters of the 1916 rebels—on your way to the Dublin Writers Museum and the Hugh Lane Municipal Gallery of Modern Art. Be sure to join the thousands of Dubliners strolling down Henry, Moore, and Mary streets, the northside's pedestrian shopping area. In the afternoon, head back to the Liffey for a quayside walk by Dublin's most imposing structure, the Custom House; then head west to the Guinness Brewery and Storehouse. Hop a bus or catch a cab back into the city and a blow-out dinner at the glamorous Tea Room in the Temple Bar's Clarence hotel. Spend the evening on a literary pub crawl to see where the likes of Beckett and Behan held court, perhaps joining a special guided tour. On the third day tour the northern outskirts of Dublin from Glasnevin Cemetery and the National Botanic Gardens across to the sublime Marino Casino in Marino and the quaint fishing village of Howth. Back in the city, have tea at Bewley's and catch a musical performance at the Olympia Theatre or a play at the Abbey Theatre.

# IF YOU HAVE FIVE DAYS

Follow the two itineraries above and then start your fourth day at Dublin's dawn—a living history of Dublin can be seen at medieval Dublinia, across the street from ancient Christ Church Cathedral, whose underground crypt is Dublin's oldest structure. Head north, jumping across the Liffey to the Four Courts, James Gandon's Georgian masterpiece and the home of the Irish judiciary. Cross back over to the south bank of the Liffey and continue westward to visit the Royal Hospital Kilmainham—the home of the Irish Museum of Modern Art— and Kilmainham Gaol, where the leaders of the Easter Rising were executed following their capture. Return via Dublin Castle, residence of British power in Ireland for nearly 800 years, and now the home of the Chester Beatty Library, containing Chinese and Turkish exhibits. On your fifth and final day explore the southern outskirts of the city, accessible by DART train, including the suburban areas of Dalkey and Sandycove (where you can visit the James Joyce Martello Tower), and the busy ferry port of Dun Laoghaire. Before returning to the city center, take a stroll along the 5-km (3-mi) beach of Sandymount Strand—that is, if Irish skies are smiling.

## In This Chapter

THE CITY CENTER: AROUND TRINITY COLLEGE 17 · THE
GEORGIAN HEART OF DUBLIN 30 · TEMPLE BAR: DUBLIN'S
"LEFT BANK" 40 · DUBLIN WEST: FROM DUBLIN CASTLE TO
THE FOUR COURTS 45 · THE LIBERTIES 57 · NORTH OF THE
LIFFEY 59 · ALONG THE GRAND CANAL 70 · PHOENIX PARK
AND ENVIRONS 73

Updated by Anto Howard

# here and there

**IN DUBLIN'S FAIR CITY** —"where the girls are so pretty" went the centuries-old ditty. Today, parts of the city—particularly the vast, uniform housing projects of the northern suburbs—may not be fair or pretty. But even if you're not conscious of it while you're in the city center, Dublin is in a beautiful setting: it loops around the edge of Dublin Bay and on a plain at the edge of the gorgeous, green Dublin and Wicklow mountains, rising softly just to the south. From the famous Four Courts building in the heart of town, the sight of the city, the bay, and the mountains will take your breath away. From the city's noted vantage points, such as the South Wall, which stretches far out into Dublin Bay, or from choice spots in the suburbs of south and north County Dublin, you can nearly get a full measure of the city. From north to south, Dublin stretches 16 km (10 mi). From its center, immediately adjacent to the port area and the River Liffey, the city spreads westward for an additional 10 km (6 mi); in total, it covers 28,000 acres. But its heart is far more compact than these numbers indicate. As in Paris, London, and Florence, and as in so many other cities throughout the world, a river runs right through Dublin. The River Liffey divides the capital into the "northside" and the "southside," as everyone calls the two principal center-city areas, and almost all the major sights in the area are well within less than an hour's walk of one another.

Coverage is organized into eight walks of the city center and the areas immediately surrounding it, and two excursions into County Dublin—the first to the southern suburbs, the latter to the northern. The first two walks—The Center City: Around

Trinity College and The Georgian Heart of Dublin—cover many of the southside's major sites: Trinity College, St. Stephen's Green, Merrion Square, and Grafton Street. It makes sense to do these walks first, as they will quickly orient you to a good portion of the southside. The third walk—Temple Bar: Dublin's "Left Bank"—takes you through this revived neighborhood, which is the hottest, hippest zone in the capital. The fourth walk— Dublin West: From Dublin Castle to the Four Courts—picks up across the street from Temple Bar and gets you to the Guinness Brewery and Storehouse, the city's most popular attraction. The fifth walk—The Liberties—takes you on a brief stroll through working-class Dublin, a historic but often overlooked part of the city. A word about these five walks: although we've split the southside into five, you'll soon realize that the distance between the areas in all these walks is not very great. The sixth walk— North of the Liffey—moves to the northside of the city center and covers all the major cultural sites there, including the James Joyce Cultural Centre, Gate Theatre, Dublin Writers Museum, and Hugh Lane Municipal Gallery of Modern Art. It also includes the rapidly developing Smithfield district, which locals are already hailing as the future "Temple Bar of the northside." The seventh walk—Along the Grand Canal—covers noteworthy sites along the canal, beginning in the northeast part of the city and ending in the southwest. Phoenix Park and Environs, at the western fringe of the northside city center, is the main focus of the eighth Dublin walk.

If you're visiting Dublin for more than two or three days, you'll probably want to explore farther afield. There's plenty to see and do a short distance from the center city—in the suburbs of both north and south County Dublin—but since you need either a car or public transportation to reach these destinations, we cover them in our Side Trips section.

Because of its compact size and traffic congestion (brought on in the last few years by an astronomical increase in the number of new vehicles), *pedestrian* traffic—especially on the city center's busiest streets during commute hours—is astonishing. Watch where you stop to consult your map or you're liable to be swept away by the ceaseless flow of the bustling crowds.

*Numbers in the text correspond to numbers in the margin and on the Dublin City Center and Dublin West maps.*

## THE CENTER CITY: AROUND TRINITY COLLEGE

The River Liffey provides a useful aid to orientation, flowing as it does through the direct middle of Dublin. If you ask a native Dubliner for directions—from under an umbrella, as it will probably be raining—he or she will most likely reply in terms of "up" or "down," up meaning away from the river or down toward it. Dublin's center of gravity had traditionally been O'Connell Bridge, a diplomatic landmark in that it avoided locating the center to the north or south of the river, as strong local loyalties still prevailed among "northsiders" (who live to the north of the river) and "southsiders," and neither would ever accept that the city's center lay on the other's side of the river. The economic boom, however, has seen diplomacy go by the wayside—Dublin's heart now beats loudest southward across the Liffey, due in part to a large-scale refurbishment and pedestrianization of Grafton Street, which made this already upscale shopping address the street to shop, stop, and be seen. At the foot of Grafton Street is the city's most famous and recognizable landmark, Trinity College; at the top of it is Dublin's most popular strolling retreat, St. Stephen's Green, a 27-acre landscaped park with flowers, lakes, bridges, and Dubliners enjoying a time-out.

## A Good Walk

*Numbers in the text correspond to numbers in the margin and on the Dublin City Center map.*

Start at **TRINITY COLLEGE** ①, exploring the quadrangle as you head to the Old Library to see the *Book of Kells*. If you want to see modern art, visit the collection housed in the Douglas Hyde Gallery, just inside the Nassau Street entrance to the college. If you're interested in the Georgian era, try to view the Provost's House and its salon, the grandest in Ireland. Trinity can easily eat up at least an hour or more, so when you come back out the front gate, you can either stop in at the **BANK OF IRELAND** ②, a neoclassic masterpiece that was once the seat of the Irish Parliament, or make an immediate left and head up **GRAFTON STREET** ③, the pedestrian spine of the southside. The **DUBLIN TOURISM** ④ office is just off Grafton Street, on the corner of Suffolk Street. If Grafton Street's shops whet your appetite for more browsing and shopping, turn right down Wicklow Street, then left up South William Street to **POWERSCOURT TOWNHOUSE CENTRE** ⑤, where a faux-Georgian atrium (very dubiously set within one of Dublin's greatest 18th-century mansions) houses high-priced shops and pleasant cafés. The **DUBLIN CIVIC MUSEUM** ⑥ is next door to Powerscourt, across the alley on its south flank. If you're doing well on time and want to explore the shopping streets farther east, jog via the alley one block east to Drury Street, from which you can access the Victorian **GEORGE'S STREET ARCADE** ⑦. Whether or not you make this excursion, you should head back to Grafton Street, where **BEWLEY'S ORIENTAL CAFÉ** ⑧, a Dublin institution, is another good place for a break. Grafton Street ends at the northwest corner of **ST. STEPHEN'S GREEN** ⑨, Dublin's most popular public gardens; they absolutely require a stroll-through. **NEWMAN HOUSE** ⑩ is on the south side of the green. Amble back across the green, exiting onto the northeast corner, at which sits the grand **SHELBOURNE MÉRIDIEN HOTEL** ⑪, a wonderful place for afternoon tea or a quick pint at one of its two pubs. The **HUGUENOT CEMETERY** ⑫ is just down the street from the hotel, on the same side. If you want to see more art, make a detour to the **RHA GALLAGHER GALLERY** ⑬.

## TIMING

Dublin's city center is so compact you could race through this walk in an hour, but in order to gain full advantage of what is on offer, set aside at least half a day—if you can—to explore the treasures of Trinity College and amble up and around Grafton Street to Stephen's Green.

## What to See

❷ **BANK OF IRELAND.** Across the street from the west facade of **Trinity College** stands one of Dublin's most striking buildings, now the Bank of Ireland but formerly the original home of the Irish Parliament. Sir Edward Lovett Pearce designed the central section in 1729; three other architects would ultimately be involved in the building's construction. A pedimented portico fronted by six massive Corinthian columns dominates the grand facade, which follows the curve of Westmoreland Street as it meets College Green, once a Viking meeting place and burial ground. Two years after the Parliament was abolished in 1801 under the Act of Union, which brought Ireland under the direct rule of Britain, the building was bought for €50,790 by the Bank of Ireland. Inside, stucco rosettes adorn the coffered ceiling in the pastel-hue, colonnaded, clerestoried **main banking hall,** at one time the Court of Requests, where citizens' petitions were heard. Just down the hall is the original **House of Lords,** with tapestries depicting the Battle of the Boyne and the Siege of Derry, an oak-paneled nave, and a 1,233-piece Waterford glass chandelier; ask a guard to show you in. Visitors are welcome during normal banking hours; the Dublin historian and author Éamonn Mac Thomáis conducts a brief guided tour every Tuesday at 10:30, 11:30, and 1:45. Accessed via Foster Place South, the small alley on the bank's east flank, the **Bank of Ireland Arts Center** frequently exhibits contemporary Irish art and has a permanent exhibition devoted to "The Story of Banking." *2 College Green, City Center, tel. 01/677–6801; 01/671–1488 arts center. €3.80. Mon.–Wed. and Fri. 10–4, Thurs. 10–5; Arts Center Tues.–Fri. 10–4, Sat. 2–5, Sun. 10–1.*

# dublin city center

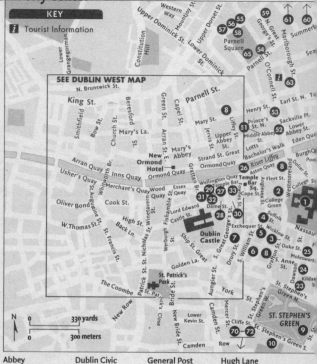

KEY

ℹ️ Tourist Information

Abbey
Presbyterian
Church, 55

The Ark, 27

Arthouse, 30

Bambrick's, 71

Bank of
Ireland, 2

Bewley's Oriental
Café, 8

Central Bank, 33

Custom
House, 64

Dublin Civic
Museum, 6

Dublin
Tourism, 4

Dublin Writers
Museum, 56

GAA Museum, 62

Gallery of
Photography, 31

Garden of
Remembrance, 58

Gate Theatre, 54

Genealogical
Office, 22

General Post
Office (GPO), 53

George's Street
Arcade, 7

Government
Buildings, 16

Grafton Street, 3

Ha'penny
Bridge, 26

Hot Press Irish
Music Hall of
Fame, 51

Hugh Lane
Municipal
Gallery of
Modern Art, 57

Huguenot
Cemetery, 12

Irish Film
Centre, 28

Irish Jewish
Museum, 70

James Joyce
Cultural
Centre, 59

Leinster
House, 18

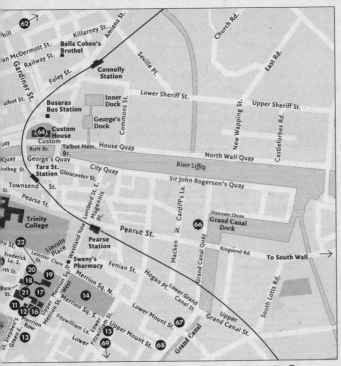

Mansion House, 23

Meeting House Square, 29

Merrion Square, 14

Mount Street Bridge, 67

Mountjoy Square, 60

National Gallery of Ireland, 19

National Library, 20

National Museum, 21

Natural History Museum, 17

Newman House, 10

Number Twenty-Nine, 15

O'Connell Street, 52

Olympia Theatre, 32

Powerscourt Townhouse Centre, 5

Pro-Cathedral, 63

RHA Gallagher Gallery, 13

Rotunda Hospital, 65

Royal Irish Academy, 24

St. Ann's Church, 25

St. Francis Xavier Church, 61

St. Stephen's Green, 9

Scruffy Murphy's, 68

Shaw Birthplace, 72

Shelbourne Méridien Hotel, 11

Statue of Patrick Kavanaugh, 69

Trinity College, 1

Waterways Visitors Centre, 66

**8 BEWLEY'S ORIENTAL CAFÉ.** The granddaddies of the capital's cafés, Bewley's has been serving coffee and buns to Dubliners since it was founded by Quakers in 1842, and now has four locations. Bewley's trademark stained-glass windows were designed by Harry Clarke (1889–1931), Ireland's most distinguished early 20th-century artist in this medium. All the branches are fine places in which to observe Dubliners of all ages and occupations. The aroma of coffee is irresistible, and the dark interiors—marble-top tables, bentwood chairs, and mahogany trim—evoke a more leisurely Dublin. The food is overpriced and not particularly good, but people-watching here over a cup of coffee or tea is a quintessential Dublin experience. (If you're interested in a more modern cup of coffee, check out the Metro Café, nearby at 43 South William Street—it's one of Dublin's best haunts for the caffeine-addicted and its staff is devoid of the devil-may-care, pseudo-existential inefficiency that seems to plague so many other Dublin cafés.) *78 Grafton St., City Center, tel. 01/677–6761 (for all locations); Sun.–Thurs. 7:30 AM–1 AM, Fri.–Sat. 7:30 AM–4 AM. 12 Westmoreland St., City Center; Mon.–Sat. 7:30 AM–9 PM, Sun. 9:30 AM–9 PM. 40 Mary St., North of the Liffey; Mon.–Wed. and Fri.–Sat. 7 AM–6 PM, Thurs. 7 AM–9 PM. Jervis Shopping Centre, Jervis and Mary Sts., North of the Liffey; Mon.–Wed. and Fri. 9 AM–6 PM, Thurs. 9 AM–9 PM, Sun. noon–6 PM.*

**6 DUBLIN CIVIC MUSEUM.** Built between 1765 and 1771 as an exhibition hall for the Society of Artists, this building later was used as the City Assembly House, precursor of City Hall. The museum's esoteric collection includes Stone Age flints, Viking coins, old maps and prints of the city, and the sculpted head of British admiral Horatio Nelson, which used to top Nelson's Pillar, beside the General Post Office on O'Connell Street; the column was toppled by an explosion in 1966 on the 50th anniversary of the Easter Uprising. The museum holds exhibitions relating to the city. *58 S. William St., City Center, tel. 01/679–4260. Free. Tues.–Sat. 10–6, Sun. 11–2.*

**④ DUBLIN TOURISM.** Churches are not just for prayers, as this deconsecrated medieval church proves. Resurrected as a visitor center, St. Andrew's, fallen into ruin after years of neglect, now houses Dublin Tourism, a private concern that offers the most complete information on Dublin's sights, restaurants, and hotels; you can even rent a car here. The office provides reservations facilities for all Dublin hotels, as well as guided tours, a plethora of brochures, and a gift shop (beware the exorbitant prices). Upstairs is a pleasant café serving sandwiches and drinks. *St. Andrew's Church, Suffolk St., City Center, tel. 01/605-7700; 1850/ 230330 (in Ireland). July–Sept., Mon.–Sat. 8:30–6, Sun. 11–5:30; Oct.– June, daily 9–6.*

**⑦ GEORGE'S STREET ARCADE.** This Victorian covered market fills the block between Drury Street to the west and South Great George's Street to the east. You'll find two dozen or so stalls selling books, prints, clothing (mostly secondhand), exotic foodstuffs, and trinkets. *S. Great George's St., City Center Mon.–Sat. 9–6.*

NEED A BREAK? In one of Dublin's most ornate traditional taverns, the **LONG HALL PUB** (51 S. Great George's St., City Center, tel. 01/475– 1590), you'll find Victorian lamps, a mahogany bar, mirrors, chandeliers, and plasterwork ceilings, all more than 100 years old. The pub serves sandwiches and an excellent pint of Guinness.

**★ ③ GRAFTON STREET.** It's no more than 200 yards long and about 20 ft wide, but brick-lined Grafton Street, open only to pedestrians, can make a claim to be the most humming street in the city, if not in all of Ireland. It is one of Dublin's vital spines: the most direct route between the front door of Trinity College and Stephen's Green, and the city's premier shopping street, home to Dublin's two most distinguished department stores, **Brown Thomas** and **Marks & Spencer.** Both on Grafton Street itself and in the smaller alleyways that radiate off it, you'll also find dozens of independent stores, a dozen or so colorful flower sellers, and some of Dublin's most popular watering holes. In summertime, buskers from all over the country and the world line both sides of the street, pouring out the sounds of drum, whistle, pipe, and string.

**⑫ HUGUENOT CEMETERY.** One of the last such burial grounds in Dublin, this cemetery was used in the late 17th century by French Protestants who had fled persecution in their native land. The cemetery gates are rarely open, but you can view the grounds from the street—it's on the northeast corner across from the square. *27 St. Stephen's Green N, City Center.*

**⑩ NEWMAN HOUSE.** One of the greatest glories of Georgian Dublin, Newman House is actually two imposing town houses joined together. The earlier of the two, No. 85 St. Stephen's Green (1738), was designed by Richard Castle, favored architect of Dublin's rich and famous, and features a winged Palladian window on the Wicklow granite facade. Originally known as Clanwilliam House, it has two landmarks of Irish Georgian style: the Apollo Room, decorated with stuccowork depicting the sun god and his muses; and the magnificent Saloon, "the supreme example of Dublin Baroque," according to scholars Jacqueline O'Brien and Desmond Guinness, crowned with an exuberant ceiling aswirl with cupids and gods, created by the Brothers Lafranchini, the finest *stuccadores* (plasterworkers) of 18th-century Dublin. Next door at No. 86 (1765), the staircase, on pastel-color walls, is one of the city's most beautiful rococo examples—with floral swags and musical instruments picked out in cake-frosting white. Catholic University (described by James Joyce in *A Portrait of the Artist as a Young Man*) was established in this building in 1850, with Cardinal John Henry Newman as its first rector. At the back of Newman House lie **Iveagh Gardens,** a delightful hideaway with statues and sunken gardens that remains one of Dublin's best-kept secrets (you can enter via Earlsfort Terrace and Harcourt Street). The Commons Restaurant is in the basement. *85–86 St. Stephen's*

Green, City Center, tel. 01/475–7255. House and garden €3.80. June–
Aug. (guided tours only), Tues.–Fri. at noon, 2, 3, and 4; Sat. at 2, 3, and
4; Sun. at 11, noon, and 1.

**⑤ POWERSCOURT TOWNHOUSE CENTRE.** Lucky man, this Viscount
Powerscourt. In the mid-18th century, not only did he build
Ireland's most spectacular country house, in Enniskerry, County
Wicklow (which bears the family name), but he also decided to
rival that structure's grandeur with one of Dublin's largest stone
mansions. Staffed with 22 servants and built of granite from the
viscount's own quarry in the Wicklow Hills, Powerscourt House
was a major statement in the Palladian style designed by Robert
Mack in 1774—a massive, Baroque-style edifice that towers over
the little street it sits on (note the top story, framed by massive
volutes, that was once intended as an observatory). The interior
decoration runs from rococo salons by James McCullagh to
Adamesque plasterwork by Michael Stapleton to—surprise—
an imaginative shopping atrium, installed in and around the
covered courtyard. The stores here include high-quality Irish
crafts shops and numerous food stalls. The mall exit leads to the
Carmelite **Church of St. Teresa's** and **Johnson's Court.** Beside
the church, a pedestrian lane leads onto Grafton Street. 59 S.
William St., City Center, tel. 01/679–4144. Mon.–Fri. 10–6, Thurs. 10–
8, Sat. 9–6, Sun. noon to 6 limited shops open.

**⑬ RHA GALLAGHER GALLERY.** The Royal Hibernian Academy, an
old Dublin institution, is housed in a well-lit building, one of the
largest exhibition spaces in the city. The gallery holds adventurous
exhibitions of the best in contemporary art, both from Ireland and
abroad. 15 Ely Pl., off St. Stephen's Green, City Center, tel. 01/661–2558.
Free. Mon.–Wed. and Fri.–Sat. 11–5, Thurs. 11–8, Sun. 2–5.

**★ ⑪ SHELBOURNE MÉRIDIEN HOTEL.** The ebullient, redbrick, white-
wood–trimmed facade of the Shelbourne has commanded "the
best address in Dublin" from the north side of St. Stephen's
Green since 1865. In 1921 the Irish Free State's constitution was
drafted here in a first-floor suite. The most financially painless

way to soak up the hotel's old-fashioned luxury and genteel excitement is to step past the entrance—note the statues of Nubian princesses and attendant slaves—for afternoon tea (€17.15 per person, including sandwiches and cakes) in the green-wallpapered **Lord Mayor's Lounge** or for a drink in one of its two bars, the **Shelbourne Bar** and the **Horseshoe Bar**, both of which are thronged with businesspeople and politicos after the workday ends. Elizabeth Bowen, famed novelist, wrote her novel *The Hotel* about this very place. *27 St. Stephen's Green, City Center, tel. 01/676–6471, www.shelbourne.ie.*

★ **9** **ST. STEPHEN'S GREEN.** Dubliners call it simply Stephen's Green, and green it is (year-round)—a verdant, 27-acre city-center square that was an open common used for the public punishment of criminals until 1664. After a long period of decline, it became a private park in 1814—the first time in its history that it was closed to the general public. Its fortunes changed again in 1880, when Sir Arthur Guinness, later Lord Ardiluan (a member of the Guinness brewery family), paid for it to be laid out anew. Flower gardens, formal lawns, a Victorian bandstand, and an ornamental lake with lots of waterfowl are all within the park's borders, connected by paths guaranteeing that strolling here or just passing through will offer up unexpected delights (palm trees). Among the park's many statues are a memorial to Yeats and another to Joyce by Henry Moore, and the *Three Fates*, a dramatic group of bronze female figures watching over man's destiny. In the 18th century the walk on the north side of the green was referred to as the Beaux Walk because most of Dublin's gentlemen's clubs were in town houses here. Today it is dominated by the **Shelbourne Méridien Hotel**. On the south side is the alluring Georgian-gorgeous Newman House. *Free. Daily sunrise–sunset.*

★ **1** **TRINITY COLLEGE.** Founded in 1592 by Queen Elizabeth I to "civilize" (Her Majesty's word) Dublin, Trinity is Ireland's oldest and most famous college. The memorably atmospheric campus is a must; here you can enjoy tracking the shadows of some of the more noted alumni, such as Jonathan Swift (1667–1745), Oscar Wilde (1854–1900), Bram Stoker (1847–1912), and Samuel Beckett (1906–89). Trinity College, Dublin (familiarly known as TCD), was founded on the site of the confiscated Priory of All Hallows. For centuries Trinity was the preserve of the Protestant church. A free education was offered to Catholics—provided that they accepted the Protestant faith. As a legacy of this condition, until 1966 Catholics who wished to study at Trinity had to obtain a dispensation from their bishop or face excommunication. Today more than 70% of Trinity's students are Catholics, an indication of how far away those days seem to today's generation.

Trinity's grounds cover 40 acres. Most of its buildings were constructed in the 18th and early 19th centuries. The extensive **West Front,** with a classical pedimented portico in the Corinthian style, faces College Green and is directly across from the **Bank of Ireland**; it was built between 1755 and 1759, and is possibly the work of Theodore Jacobsen, architect of London's Foundling Hospital. The design is repeated on the interior, so the view is the same both from outside the gates and from the quadrangle inside. On the lawn in front of the inner facade are **statues** of orator Edmund Burke (1729–97) and dramatist Oliver Goldsmith (1728–74), two other alumni. Like the West Front, **Parliament Square** (commonly known as Front Square), the cobblestoned quadrangle that lies just beyond this first patch of lawn, also dates from the 18th century. On the right side of the square is Sir William Chambers's **theater,** or **Examination Hall,** dating from the mid-1780s, which contains the college's most splendid Adamesque interior (designed by Michael Stapleton). The hall houses an impressive organ retrieved from an 18th-century Spanish ship and a gilded oak chandelier from the old House of Commons; concerts are sometimes held here. The **chapel,** which stands on the left of the quadrangle, has stucco ceilings and fine woodwork. Both the theater and the chapel were designed by Scotsman William Chambers in the late 18th century. The looming **Campanile,** or bell tower, is the symbolic heart of the college; erected in 1853, it dominates the center of the square. To the left of the campanile is the **Graduates Memorial Building**, or GMB. Built in 1892, the slightly Gothic building is now home to both the Philosophical and Historical Societies, Trinity's ancient and fiercely competitive debating groups. At the back of the square stands old redbrick **Rubrics**, looking rather ordinary and out of place among the gray granite and cobblestones. Rubrics, now used as rooms for students and faculty, dates from 1690, making it the oldest building still standing.

Ireland's largest collection of books and manuscripts is housed in **Trinity College Library.** Its principal treasure is the *Book of Kells,* generally considered the most striking manuscript ever produced in the Anglo-Saxon world and one of the greatest masterpieces of early Christian art. Once thought to be lost— the Vikings looted the book in 1007 for its jeweled cover but ultimately left the manuscript behind—the book is a splendidly illuminated version of the Gospels. In the 12th century, Guardius Cambensis declared that the book was made by an angel's hand in answer to a prayer of St. Bridget; in the 20th century, scholars decided instead that the book originated on the island of Iona in Scotland, where followers of St. Colomba lived until the island came under siege in the early to mid-9th century. They fled to Kells, County Meath, bringing the book with them. The 680-page work was rebound in four volumes in 1953, two of which are usually displayed at a time, so you typically see no more than four original pages. (Some wags have taken to calling it the "Page of Kells.") However, such is the incredible workmanship of the *Book of Kells* that one folio contains the equivalent of many other manuscripts. On some pages, it has been determined that within a quarter inch, no fewer than 158 interlacements of a ribbon pattern of white lines on a black background can be discerned—little wonder some historians feel this book contains all the designs to be found in Celtic art. Note, too, the extraordinary colors, some of which were derived from shellfish, beetles' wings, and crushed pearls. The most famous page shows the "XPI" monogram (symbol of Christ), but if this page is not on display, you can still see a replica of it, and many of the other lavishly illustrated pages, in the adjacent exhibition—dedicated to the history, artistry, and conservation of the book—through which you must pass to see the originals.

Because of the fame and beauty of the *Book of Kells*, it is all too easy to overlook the other treasures in the library. They include the *Book of Armagh*, a 9th-century copy of the New Testament that also contains St. Patrick's Confession, and the legendary *Book of Durrow*, a 7th-century Gospel book from County Offaly. You may have to wait in line to enter the library; it's less busy early in the day.

The **Old Library,** aptly known as the Long Room, is one of Dublin's most staggering sights. It's 213 ft long and 42 ft wide, and contains in its 21 alcoves approximately 200,000 of the 3 million volumes in Trinity's collection. Originally the room had a flat plaster ceiling, but in 1859–60 the need for more shelving resulted in a decision to raise the level of the roof and add the barrel-vaulted ceiling and the gallery bookcases. Since the 1801 Copyright Act, the college has received a copy of every book published in Britain and Ireland, and a great number of these publications must be stored in other parts of the campus and beyond. Of note are the carved Royal Arms of Queen Elizabeth I, above the library entrance—the only surviving relic of the original college buildings—and, lining the Long Room, a grand series of marble busts, of which the most famous is Roubiliac's portrait of Jonathan Swift. The Trinity College Library Shop sells books, clothing, jewelry, and postcards. *City Center, tel. 01/608–2308, www.tcd.ie. €5.70 for the Long Room. June–Sept., Mon.–Sat. 9:30–5, Sun. 9:30–4:30; Oct.–May, Mon.–Sat. 9:30–5, Sun. noon–4:30.*

Trinity College's stark, modern Arts and Social Sciences Building, with an entrance on Nassau Street, houses the **Douglas Hyde Gallery of Modern Art,** which concentrates on contemporary art exhibitions and has its own bookstore. Also in the building, down some steps from the gallery, there's a snack bar with coffee, tea, sandwiches, and students willing to talk about life in the old college. *tel. 01/608–1116. Free. Mon.–Wed. and Fri. 11–6, Thurs. 11–7, Sat. 11–4:45.*

The **New Berkeley Library,** the main student library at Trinity, was built in 1967 and named after the philosopher and alumnus George Berkeley. The small open space in front of the library contains a spherical brass sculpture designed by Arnaldo Pomodoro. The library is not open to the general public. *College Green, tel. 01/677–2941. Grounds daily 8 AM–10 PM.*

In the Thomas Davis Theatre in the arts building, the **"Dublin Experience,"** a 45-minute audiovisual presentation, explains the history of the city over the last 1,000 years. *tel. 01/608–1688. €3.80; in conjunction with Old Library, €7.60. Late-May–Oct., daily 10–5; shows every hr on the hr.*

## THE GEORGIAN HEART OF DUBLIN

If there's one travel poster that signifies "Dublin" more than any other, it's the one that pictures 50 or so Georgian doorways— door after colorful door, all graced with lovely fanlights upheld by columns. A building boom began in Dublin in the early 18th century as the Protestant ascendancy constructed town houses for themselves and civic structures for their city in the style that came to be known as Georgian, for the four successive British Georges who ruled from 1714 through 1830. The Georgian architectural rage owed much to architects like James Gandon and Richard Castle. They and others were influenced by Andrea Palladio (1508–80), whose *Four Books of Architecture* were published in the 1720s in London and helped to precipitate the revival of his style, which swept through England and its colonies. Never again would Dublin be so "smart," so filled with decorum and style, nor its visitors' book so full of aristocratic names. Note that while Dublin's southside is a veritable shop window of the Georgian style, there are many other period sights to be found northside—for instance, the august interiors of the Dublin Writers Museum and Belvedere College, or James Gandon's great civic structures, the Custom House and the Four Courts, found quayside. These, and other Georgian goodies, are described in the Exploring sections of Dublin West and North of the Liffey.

## A Good Walk

*Numbers in the text correspond to numbers in the margin and on the Dublin City Center map.*

When Dublin was transformed into a Georgian metropolis, people came from all over to admire the new pillared and corniced city. Today, walking through Fitzwilliam Square or Merrion Street Upper, you can still admire vistas of calm Georgian splendor. Begin your Palladian promenade at the northeast corner of Stephen's Green—here, in front of the men's clubs, was the Beaux Walk, a favorite 18th-century gathering place for fashionable Dubliners. Chances are you won't bump into a duke on his way to a Handel concert or an earl on his way to a rout, ball, and supper, but then, you won't have to dodge pigs either, which used to dot the cityscape back then. Walk down Merrion Street to **MERRION SQUARE** ⑭—one of Dublin's most attractive squares. The east side of Merrion Square and its continuation, Fitzwilliam Street, form what is known as "the Georgian mile," which, unlike some Irish miles, actually measures less than a kilometer. On a clear day the Dublin Mountains are visible in the distance and the prospect has almost (thanks to the ugly, modern office block of the Electricity Supply Board) been preserved to give an impression of the spacious feel of 18th-century Dublin. Walk down the south side of the square to **NUMBER TWENTY-NINE** ⑮. Cut back through the square to visit the refurbished **GOVERNMENT BUILDINGS** ⑯, the **NATURAL HISTORY MUSEUM** ⑰, **LEINSTER HOUSE** ⑱, and/or the **NATIONAL GALLERY OF IRELAND** ⑲. The last leg of this walk is up Kildare Street to the **NATIONAL LIBRARY** ⑳, passing the back of Leinster House to the **NATIONAL MUSEUM** ㉑. Stop in at the **GENEALOGICAL OFFICE** ㉒ if you're doing research about your ancestors. Walk back to Stephen's Green and down Harrington Street to Synge Street and the **SHAW BIRTHPLACE** ㉒. Return to the Green and go down Dawson Street, which runs parallel to Grafton Street. The **MANSION HOUSE** ㉓, **ROYAL IRISH ACADEMY** ㉔, and **ST. ANN'S CHURCH** ㉕ are on the left as you walk down toward Trinity College's side entrance.

### TIMING

Dublin is so compact you could race through this walk in two hours, if you don't linger anywhere or set foot in one of the museums. But the treasures at the National Gallery and the National Museum, and the green tranquillity of Merrion Square, may slow you down. Many of Dublin's finest sites along the way, and dozens of the city's most historic pubs, may also entice you. So, if you don't get too distracted, do this walk over the course of a half-day.

## What to See

㉒ **GENEALOGICAL OFFICE.** Are you a Fitzgibbon from Limerick, a Cullen from Waterford, or a McSweeney from Cork? This reference library is a good place to begin your ancestor-tracing efforts. If you're a total novice at genealogical research, you can meet with an advisor (€31.75 for an hour consultation) who can help get you started. It also houses the **Heraldic Museum,** where displays of flags, coins, stamps, silver, and family crests highlight the uses and development of heraldry in Ireland. Note that a map detailing the geographical origin of the hundred or so most common Irish surnames can be found at the back of this book. *2 Kildare St., City Center, tel. 01/661–4877, www.nli.ie. Free. Genealogical Office weekdays 10–12:30 and 2–4:30, Sat. 10–12:30; Heraldic Museum weekdays 10–8:30, Sat. 10–12:30. Guided tours by appointment.*

**16 GOVERNMENT BUILDINGS.** The swan song of British architecture in the capital, this enormous complex was the last neoclassical edifice to be erected by the British government. A landmark of "Edwardian Baroque," it was designed by Sir Aston Webb (who did many of the similarly grand buildings in London's Piccadilly Circus) as the College of Science in the early 1900s. Following a major restoration, these buildings became the offices of the Department of the *taoiseach* (the prime minister, pronounced *tea*-shuck) and the *tánaiste* (the deputy prime minister, pronounced tawn-ish-ta). Fine examples of contemporary Irish furniture and carpets populate the offices. A stained-glass window, known as "My Four Green Fields," was originally made by Evie Hone for the 1939 World Trade Fair in New York. It depicts the four ancient provinces of Ireland: Munster, Ulster, Leinster, and Connacht. The government offices are accessible only via 45-minute guided tours given on Saturday (tickets are available on the day of the tour from the National Gallery), though they are dramatically illuminated every night. *Upper Merrion St., City Center, tel.* 01/662–4888. *Free. Sat.* 10:30–3:30.

**18 LEINSTER HOUSE.** Commissioned by the Duke of Leinster and built in 1745, this residence almost single-handedly ignited the Georgian style that dominated Dublin for 100 years. It was not only the largest private home in the city but Richard Castle's first structure in Ireland (Castle, a follower of Palladio, designed some of the country's most important Palladian country houses). Inside, the grand salons were ornamented with coffered ceilings, Rembrandts, and Van Dycks, fitting settings for the parties often given by the duke's wife (and celebrated beauty), Lady Emily Lennox. The building has two facades: the one facing Merrion Square is designed in the style of a country house; the other, on Kildare Street, resembles that of a town house. This latter facade—if you ignore the ground-floor level—was a major inspiration for Irishman James Hoban's designs for the White House in Washington, D.C. Built in hard Ardbracan limestone, the house's exterior makes a cold impression, and, in fact, the duke's heirs pronounced the house "melancholy" and fled. Today, the house is the seat of Dáil Éireann (the House of Representatives, pronounced dawl e-rin) and Seanad Éireann (the Senate, pronounced shanad e-rin), which together constitute the Irish Parliament. When the Dáil is not in session, tours can be arranged weekdays; when the Dáil is in session, tours are available only on Monday and Friday. The Dáil visitors' gallery is included in the tour, although it can be accessed on days when the Dáil is in session and tours are not available. To arrange a visit, contact the public relations office at the phone number provided. *Kildare St., City Center, tel. 01/618–3000, www.irlgov.ie. Free*

**㉓ MANSION HOUSE.** The mayor of Dublin resides at the Mansion House, which dates from 1710. It was built for Joshua Dawson, who later sold the property to the government on condition that "one loaf of double refined sugar of six pounds weight" be delivered to him every Christmas. In 1919 the Declaration of Irish Independence was adopted here. Dawson Street (named for the house's original tenant) is the site of the annual and popular **August Antiques Fair.** The house is not open to the public. *Dawson St., City Center.*

★ **⑭ MERRION SQUARE.** Created between 1762 and 1764, this tranquil square a few blocks to the east of St. Stephen's Green is lined on three sides by some of Dublin's best-preserved Georgian town houses, many of which have brightly painted front doors crowned by intricate fanlights. Leinster House—Dublin's Versailles—and the Natural History Museum and National Gallery line the west side of the square. It's on the other sides, however, that the Georgian terrace streetscape comes into its own—the finest houses are on the north border. Even when its flower gardens are not in bloom, the vibrant, mostly evergreen grounds, dotted with sculpture and threaded with meandering paths, are worth a walk-through. The square has been the home of several distinguished Dubliners, including Oscar Wilde's parents, Sir William and "Speranza" Wilde (No. 1); Irish national leader Daniel

O'Connell (No. 58); and authors W. B. Yeats (Nos. 52 and 82) and Sheridan LeFanu (No. 70). Walk past the houses and read the plaques on the house facades, which identify the former inhabitants. Until 50 years ago, the square was a fashionable residential area, but today most of the houses are offices. At the south end of Merrion Square, on Upper Mount Street, stands **St. Stephen's Church** (Church of Ireland). Known locally as the "pepper canister" church because of its cupola, the structure was inspired in part by Wren's churches in London. *South of the Liffey. Daily sunrise–sunset.*

★ ⑲ **NATIONAL GALLERY OF IRELAND.** Caravaggio's *The Taking of Christ* (1602), Reynolds's *First Earl of Bellamont* (1773), Vermeer's *Lady Writing a Letter with Her Maid* (ca. 1670) . . . you get the picture. The National Gallery of Ireland—the first in a series of major civic buildings on the west side of Merrion Square—is one of Europe's finest smaller art museums, with more than 3,000 works. Unlike Europe's largest art museums, which are almost guaranteed to induce Stendhal's syndrome, the National Gallery can be thoroughly covered in a morning or afternoon without inducing exhaustion. An 1854 Act of Parliament provided for the establishment of the museum, which was helped along by William Dargan (1799–1867), who was responsible for building much of Ireland's railway network in the 19th century (he is honored by a statue on the front lawn). The 1864 building was designed by Francis Fowke, who was also responsible for London's Victoria & Albert Museum.

A highlight of the museum is the major collection of paintings by Irish artists from the 17th through 20th centuries, including works by Roderic O'Conor (1860–1940), Sir William Orpen (1878–1931), William Leech (1881–1968), and Jack B. Yeats (1871–1957), the brother of W. B. Yeats and by far the best-known Irish painter of the 20th century. Yeats painted portraits and landscapes in an abstract expressionist style not unlike that of the later Bay Area Figurative painters of the 1950s and 1960s.

His *The Liffey Swim* (1923) is particularly worth seeing for its Dublin subject matter (the annual swim is still held, usually on the first weekend in September).

The collection also claims exceptional paintings from the 17th-century French, Dutch, Italian, and Spanish schools. Among the highlights that you should strive to see are those mentioned above (the spectacular Caravaggio made headlines around the world when it was found hanging undiscovered in a Jesuit house not far from the museum) and Rembrandt's *Rest on the Flight into Egypt* (1647), Poussin's *The Holy Family* (1649) and *Lamentation over the Dead Christ* (ca. 1655–60), and, somewhat later than these, Goya's *Portrait of Doña Antonia Zárate* (circa 1810). Don't forget to check out the portrait of the First Earl of Bellamont, by Reynolds; the earl was among the first to introduce the Georgian fashion to Ireland, and this portrait stunningly flaunts the extraordinary style of the man himself. The French Impressionists are represented with paintings by Monet, Sisley, and Pissarro. The northern wing of the gallery houses the British collection and the Irish National Portrait collection, and the amply stocked **gift shop** is a good place to pick up books on Irish artists. In January 2002, the spectacular new Millennium Wing, a standout of postmodern architecture in Dublin, opened. The wing also houses part of the permanent collection, and will be used to stage major international travelling shows. Free guided tours are available on Saturday at 3 PM and on Sunday at 2, 3, and 4. *Merrion Sq. W, City Center, tel. 01/661–5133, www.nationalgallery.ie. Free. Mon.–Wed. and Fri.–Sat. 9:30–5:30, Thurs. 9:30–8:30, Sun. 12–5:30.*

**NEED A BREAK?** **FITZER'S** (*Merrion Sq. W, South of the Liffey, tel. 01/661–4496*), the National Gallery's self-service restaurant, is a find—one of the city's best spots for an inexpensive, top-rate lunch. The 16 to 20 daily menu items are prepared with an up-to-date take on new European cuisine. It's open Monday–Saturday 10–5:30 (lunch is served noon–2:30), and Sunday 2–5.

**②⓪ NATIONAL LIBRARY.** Ireland is one of the few countries in the world where one can happily admit to being a writer. And few countries as geographically diminutive as Ireland have garnered as many recipients of the Nobel Prize for Literature. Along with works by W. B. Yeats (1923), George Bernard Shaw (1925), Samuel Beckett (1969), and Seamus Heaney (1995), the National Library contains first editions of every major Irish writer, including books by Jonathan Swift, Oliver Goldsmith, and James Joyce (who used the library as the scene of the great literary debate in *Ulysses*). In addition, of course, almost every book ever published in Ireland is kept here, as well as an unequaled selection of old maps and an extensive collection of Irish newspapers and magazines— more than 5 million items in all. The main **Reading Room** opened in 1890 to house the collections of the Royal Dublin Society. Beneath its dramatic domed ceiling, countless authors have researched and written their books over the years. *Kildare St., City Center, tel. 01/661–8811, www.nli.ie. Free. Mon.–Wed. 10–9, Thurs.– Fri. 10–5, Sat. 10–1.*

★ **②① NATIONAL MUSEUM.** On the other side of Leinster House from the National Library, Ireland's National Museum houses a fabled collection of Irish artifacts, dating from 7000 BC to the present. The museum is organized around a grand rotunda and elaborately decorated, with mosaic floors, marble columns, balustrades, and fancy ironwork. It has the largest collection of Celtic antiquities in the world, including an array of gold jewelry, carved stones, bronze tools, and weapons. The Treasury collection, including some of the museum's most renowned pieces, is open on a permanent basis. Among the priceless relics on display are the 8th-century **Ardagh Chalice,** a two-handle silver cup with gold filigree ornamentation; the bronze-coated, iron **St. Patrick's Bell,** the oldest surviving example (5th–8th centuries) of Irish metalwork; the 8th-century **Tara Brooch,** an intricately decorated piece made of white bronze, amber, and glass; and the 12th-century bejeweled oak **Cross of Cong,** covered with silver and bronze panels. The Road to Independence Room is devoted to the 1916 Easter Uprising and the War of Independence (1919–21); displays here include uniforms, weapons, banners, and a piece of the flag that flew over the General Post Office during Easter Week, 1916. Upstairs, Viking Age Ireland is a permanent exhibit on the Norsemen, featuring a full-size Viking skeleton, swords, leather works recovered in Dublin and surrounding areas, and a replica of a small Viking boat. In contrast to the ebullient late-Victorian architecture of the main museum building, the design of the **National Museum Annexe** is purely functional; it houses temporary shows of Irish antiquities. The 18th-century **Collins Barracks,** near the Phoenix Park, houses a collection of glass, silver, furniture, and other decorative arts. *Kildare St.; Annexe: 7– 9 Merrion Row, City Center; tel. 01/677–7444, www.museum.ie. Free. Tues.–Sat. 10–5, Sun. 2–5.*

⑰ **NATURAL HISTORY MUSEUM.** The famed explorer of the African interior, Dr. Stanley Livingstone (recall the expression, "Dr. Livingstone, I presume?") inaugurated this museum when it opened in 1857. Today, it is little changed from Victorian times and remains a fascinating repository of mounted mammals, birds, and other flora and fauna. The Irish Room houses the most famous exhibits, skeletons of Ireland's extinct, prehistoric giant "Irish elk." The World Animals Collection includes a 65-ft whale skeleton suspended from the roof. Don't miss the very beautiful Blaschka Collection, finely detailed glass models of marine creatures, the zoological accuracy of which has never been achieved since. The museum is next door to the **Government Buildings.** *Merrion Sq. W, City Center, tel. 01/677–7444, www. museum.ie. Free. Tues.–Sat. 10–5, Sun. 2–5.*

⑮ **NUMBER TWENTY-NINE.** Everything in this carefully refurbished 1794 home, known simply as Number Twenty-Nine, is in keeping with the elegant lifestyle of the Dublin middle class between 1790 and 1820, the height of the Georgian period, when the house was owned by a wine merchant's widow. From the basement to the attic, in the kitchen, nursery, servant's quarters, and the formal living areas, the National Museum of Ireland has re-created the period's style with authentic furniture, paintings, carpets, curtains, paint, wallpapers, and even bellpulls. *29 Lower Fitzwilliam St., South of the Liffey, tel. 01/702–6165. €3.15. Tues.–Sat. 10–5, Sun. 2–5.*

**㉔ ROYAL IRISH ACADEMY.** Adjacent to the **Mansion House,** the country's leading learned society houses important manuscripts in its 18th-century library, including a large collection of ancient Irish manuscripts, such as the 11th- to 12th-century *Book of the Dun Cow,* and the library of the 18th-century poet Thomas Moore. *19 Dawson St., City Center, tel. 01/676–2570, www.ria.ie. Free. Weekdays 9:30–5.*

**㉕ ST. ANN'S CHURCH.** St. Ann's plain, neo-Romanesque granite exterior, built in 1868, belies the Church of Ireland's rich Georgian interior, which Isaac Wills designed in 1720. Highlights of the interior include polished-wood balconies, ornate plasterwork, and shelving in the chancel dating from 1723—and still in use for distributing bread to the parish's poor. *Dawson St., City Center, tel. 01/676–7727, Free. Weekdays 10–4, Sun. for services.*

**㉛ SHAW BIRTHPLACE.** "Author of many plays" is the simple accolade to George Bernard Shaw on the plaque outside his birthplace. The Nobel laureate was born here in 1856 to a once prosperous family fallen on harder times. Shaw lived in this modest, Victorian terrace house until he was 10 and remembers it as having a "loveless" feel. The painstaking restoration of the little rooms highlights the cramped, claustrophobic atmosphere. All the details of a family home—wallpaper, paint, fittings, curtains, furniture, utensils, pictures, rugs—remain, and it appears as if the family has just gone out for the afternoon. You can almost hear one of Mrs. Shaw's musical recitals in the tiny front parlor. The children's bedrooms are dotted with photographs and original documents and letters that throw light on Shaw's career. *33 Synge St., South of the Liffey, tel. 01/475–0854. €5.50. Apr.–Oct., Mon.–Sat. 10–5, Sun. 11–5.*

## TEMPLE BAR: DUBLIN'S "LEFT BANK"

More than any other neighborhood in Dublin, Temple Bar represents the dramatic changes (good and bad) and ascending fortunes of Dublin in the last 10 years. Named after one of the streets of its central spine, the area was targeted for redevelopment in 1991–92 after a long period of neglect, having survived widely rumored plans to turn it into a massive bus depot and/or a giant parking lot. Temple Bar took off fast into Dublin's version of New York's SoHo, Paris's Bastille, London's Notting Hill—a thriving mix of high and alternative culture distinct from that you'll find in every other part of the city. Dotting the area's narrow cobblestone streets and pedestrian alleyways are new apartment buildings (inside they tend to be small and uninspired, with sky-high rent), vintage-clothing stores, postage-stamp–size boutiques selling €250 sunglasses and other expensive gewgaws, art galleries galore, a hotel resuscitated by U2, hip restaurants, pubs, clubs, European-style cafés, and a smattering of cultural venues. Visit the Temple Bar Web site (www.temple-bar.ie) for information about events in the area.

Temple Bar's regeneration was no doubt abetted by that one surefire real estate asset: location, location, location. The area is bordered by Dame Street to the south, the Liffey to the north, Fishamble Street to the west, and Westmoreland Street to the east. In fact, Temple Bar is so perfectly situated between everywhere else in Dublin that it's difficult to believe this neighborhood was once largely forsaken. It's now sometimes called the "playing ground of young Dublin," and for good reason: on weekend evenings and daily in the summer it teems with young people—not only from Dublin but from all over Europe—who fly into the city for the weekend, drawn by its pubs, clubs, and lively craic. It has become a favorite of young Englishmen on "stag" weekends, 48-hour bachelor parties heavy on drinking and debauching. Some who have witnessed Temple Bar's rapid gentrification and commercialization complain that it's losing its artistic soul—*Harper's Bazaar* said it was in danger of becoming "a sort of pseudoplace," like London's Covent Garden Piazza or Paris's Les Halles. Over the next few years the planned Smithfield development may replace Temple Bar at the cutting edge of Dublin culture, but for the moment there's no denying that this is one of the best places to get a handle on the city.

## A Good Walk

*Numbers in the text correspond to numbers in the margin and on the Dublin City Center map.*

Start at O'Connell Bridge and walk down Aston Quay, taking in the terrific view west down the River Liffey. Alleys and narrow roads to your left lead into Temple Bar, but hold off turning in until you get to **HA'PENNY BRIDGE** ㉖, a Liffey landmark. Turn right and walk through Merchant's Arch, the symbolic entry into Temple Bar (see if you can spot the surveillance cameras up on the walls), which leads you onto the area's long spine, named Temple Bar here but also called Fleet Street (to the east) and Essex Street (both east and west, to the west). You're right at Temple Bar Square, one of the two largest plazas in Temple Bar. Just up on the right are two of the area's leading art galleries, the Temple Bar Gallery (at Lower Fownes Street) and, another block up, the Original Print Gallery and Black Church Print Studios. Turn left onto Eustace Street. If you have children, you may want to go to the **ARK** ㉗, a children's cultural center. Across the street from the Ark, stop in at the Temple Bar Information Centre and pick up a handy *Temple Bar Guide*. Farther down Eustace Street is the **IRISH FILM CENTRE** ㉘, Temple Bar's leading cultural venue and a great place to catch classic or new indie films. In summer, the IFC organizes Saturday-night outdoor screenings on **MEETING HOUSE SQUARE** ㉙, behind the Ark, accessed via Curved Street. The street is dominated on one side by the **ARTHOUSE** ㉚ and on the other by the Temple Bar Music Centre.

Dublin's leading photography gallery, the **GALLERY OF PHOTOGRAPHY** ㉛, is also here. Walk a few steps west to the narrow, cobbled Sycamore Street, and then turn right and walk to Dame Street, where you'll find the **OLYMPIA THEATRE** ㉜. Farther down Dame Street, the ultramodern **CENTRAL BANK** ㉝ rises above the city. Head for the corner of Parliament Street, where you can stop for a break or begin the next walk.

**TIMING**

You can easily breeze through Temple Bar in an hour or so, but if you've got the time, plan to spend a morning or afternoon here, drifting in and out of the dozens of stores and galleries, relaxing at a café over a cup of coffee or at a pub over a pint, or maybe even watching a film, if you're looking for a change from sightseeing.

## What to See

㉗ **THE ARK.** If you're traveling with children and looking for something fun to do, stop by the Ark, Ireland's children's cultural center, housed in a former Presbyterian church. Its theater opens onto Meeting House Square for outdoor performances in summer. A gallery and workshop space host ongoing activities. *Eustace St., Temple Bar, tel. 01/670–7788, www.ark.ie. Free. Weekdays 9:30–5:30, weekends only if there is a show.*

㉚ **ARTHOUSE.** If you're a fan of the art of the digital age, you'll love this place. If not, skip it. Arthouse is one of the first multimedia centers for the arts in the world. Its modern design—glass, metal, and painted concrete—is the work of architect Shay Cleary Doyle, who wanted the building to reflect the object glorified within: the computer. Inside are a training center, a performance venue, a creative studio, and an exhibition space that hosts art exhibitions. Pride of place, however, goes to the Art Information Bureau and the Artifact artist's database, which features the work of more than 1,000 modern Irish artists working in Ireland and abroad. This useful catalog is open to anyone who wants to buy or admire the work of the listed artists. You can search for work according to specific criteria—you press a few buttons and a list of artists and images of their work fitting your description will appear. *Curved St., Temple Bar, tel. 01/605–6800, www.arthouse.ie. Free. Weekdays 9–6.*

**33** **CENTRAL BANK.** Everyone in Dublin seems to have an opinion on the Central Bank. Designed by Sam Stephenson in 1978, the controversial, ultramodern glass-and-concrete building suspends huge concrete slabs around a central axis. It was originally one floor taller, but that had to be lopped off as a hazard to low-flying planes. Skateboarders and in-line skaters have taken up residence on the little plaza in front of the building. *Dame St., Temple Bar, tel. 01/671–6666, www.centralbank.ie. Free. Weekdays 10–6.*

**31** **GALLERY OF PHOTOGRAPHY.** Dublin's premier photography gallery has a permanent collection of early 20th-century Irish photography and also puts on monthly exhibits of contemporary Irish and international photographers. The gallery is an invaluable social record of Ireland. The bookstore is the best place in town to browse for photography books and pick up arty postcards. *Meeting House Sq. S, Temple Bar, tel. 01/671–4654, www. irish-photography.com. Free. Tues.–Sat. 11–6.*

**26** **HA'PENNY BRIDGE.** Every Dubliner has a story about meeting someone on this cast-iron Victorian bridge, a heavily trafficked footbridge that crosses the Liffey at a prime spot—Temple Bar is on the south side, and the bridge provides the fastest route to the thriving Mary and Henry Street shopping areas to the north. Until early in the 20th century, a half-penny toll was charged to cross it. Yeats was one among many Dubliners who found this too high a price to pay—more a matter of principle than of finance—and so made the detour via O'Connell Bridge. Congestion on the Ha'penny has been relieved with the opening of the Millennium Footbridge a few hundred yards up the river. In a major renovation in 2001 the old bridge was cleaned and returned to its original sparkling white.

**28 IRISH FILM CENTRE (IFC).** The opening of the IFC in a former Quaker meetinghouse helped to launch the revitalization of Temple Bar. It has two comfortable art-house cinemas showing revivals and new independent films, the Irish Film Archive, a bookstore for cineastes, and a popular bar and restaurant/café, all of which makes this one of the neighborhood's most vital cultural institutions and the place to be seen. *6 Eustace St., Temple Bar, tel. 01/679–5744, www.fii.ie. Free. Weekdays 9:30–late, weekends 11–late.*

NEED A
BREAK? The trendy **IRISH FILM CENTRE CAFÉ** (6 Eustace St., Temple Bar, tel. 01/679–5744) is a pleasant place for a lunchtime break. Sandwiches are large and healthful, with plenty of nonmeat choices, and the people-watching is nonpareil.

**29 MEETING HOUSE SQUARE.** Behind the Ark and accessed via Curved Street, the square gets its name from a nearby Quaker meetinghouse. Now it's something of a gathering place for Dublin's youth and artists. A variety of summer events—classic movies (every Saturday night), theater, games, and family programs—take place here. (Thankfully, seats are installed.) The Square is also a favorite site for the continuously changing street sculpture that pops up all over Temple Bar (artists commissioned by the city sometimes create oddball pieces, such as a half of a Volkswagon protruding from a wall). But year-round, the Square is a great spot to sit, people-watch, and take in the sounds of the buskers (street musicians) who swarm to the place. There's also an organic food market here every Saturday morning.

★ **32 OLYMPIA THEATRE.** One of the best places anywhere in Europe to see live musical acts, the Olympia is Dublin's second oldest and one of its busiest theaters. Built in 1879, this classic Victorian music hall has a gorgeous red wrought-iron facade. Conveniently, you'll find two pubs here—through doors directly off the back of the theater's orchestra section. The Olympia's long-standing

Friday and Saturday series, "Midnight at the Olympia," has brought a wide array of musical performers to Dublin, and the theater has also seen many notable actors strut on its stage, including Alec Guinness, Peggy Ashcroft, Noël Coward, and even Laurel and Hardy. Big-name performers like Van Morrison often choose the intimate atmosphere of the Olympia over a larger venue. It's really a hot place to see some fine performances, so if you have a chance, by all means go. *72 Dame St., Temple Bar, tel. 01/677-7744.*

NEED A BREAK? The creamiest, frothiest coffees in all of Temple Bar can be had at the **JOY OF COFFEE/IMAGE GALLERY CAFÉ** (25 E. Essex St., Temple Bar, tel. 01/679-3393); the wall of windows floods light onto the small gallery with original photographs adorning the walls.

## DUBLIN WEST: FROM DUBLIN CASTLE TO THE FOUR COURTS

This section of Dublin takes you from the 10th-century crypt at Christ Church Cathedral—the city's oldest surviving structure—to the modern plant of the Guinness Brewery and its Storehouse museum. It also crosses the Liffey for a visit to Smithfield, the old market area being billed as the next hot location in the city. Dublin is so compact, however, that to separate out the following sites from those covered in the two other city-center southside walks is potentially to mislead—by suggesting that this area is at some remove from the heart of the city center. In fact, this tour's starting point, City Hall, is just across the street from Thomas Read's, and Christ Church Cathedral is a very short walk farther west. The westernmost sites covered here—notably the Royal Hospital and Kilmainham Gaol—are, however, at some distance, so if you're not an enthusiastic walker, you may want to drive or catch a cab or a bus out to them.

## A Good Walk

*Numbers in the text correspond to numbers in the margin and on the Dublin West map.*

Begin with a brief visit to **CITY HALL** ㉞, and then walk up Cork Hill to the Castle Street entrance to **DUBLIN CASTLE** ㉟, whose highlights—the grand salons that show off Viceregal Dublin at its most splendid—are only visitable via a guided tour. In the castle you'll also find the **CHESTER BEATTY LIBRARY** ㊱, a world-renowned collection of Oriental art and manuscripts. Leave via the same gate, turn left, and walk up Castle Street to the ancient, picturesque **CHRIST CHURCH CATHEDRAL** ㊲, on one of the city's few hills. At the southeast corner of the cathedral, connected via an utterly beguiling Victorian-era bridge, **DUBLINIA** ㊳ gives you a chance to experience life in medieval Dublin. Just down Nicholas Street is—begorrah!—**ST. PATRICK'S CATHEDRAL** ㊴. If you're eager to venture back to the 17th century or love old books, visit the quaint **MARSH'S LIBRARY** ㊵, next door to St. Patrick's. You can then stroll through the old artisan redbrick dwellings in the Liberties, home to the heaviest concentration of the city's antiques stores, to Thomas Street and—just follow your nose—the **GUINNESS BREWERY AND STOREHOUSE** ㊶, where you can keep your spirits up in more ways than one. At this point, if you want to see more architecture and modern art, proceed farther west to the Irish Museum of Modern Art in the elegant 18th-century **ROYAL HOSPITAL KILMAINHAM** ㊷, and the **KILMAINHAM GAOL** ㊸. If you don't elect to head this way, turn back down Thomas Street, crossing the Liffey at Bridge Street, which on its north side becomes Church Street. On your left is the **FOUR COURTS** ㊹. A little farther up on the left is **ST. MICHAN'S CHURCH** ㊺ and the beginning of the Smithfield area. A quick jog over to Bow Street (via Mary's Lane) brings you to the **OLD JAMESON DISTILLERY** ㊻—here you'll learn all there is to learn about Irish whiskey. End your walk with a thrilling ride up the glass elevator to the top of **THE CHIMNEY** ㊼.

**TIMING**

Allow yourself a few hours, especially if you want to include the Guinness Brewery and Storehouse and the Irish Museum of Modern Art at the Royal Hospital. Keep in mind that if you want to cover the easternmost sites—Dublin Castle, City Hall, Christ Church Cathedral, and environs—you can easily append them to a tour of Temple Bar.

## What to See

★ ㊱ **CHESTER BEATTY LIBRARY.** After Sir Alfred Chester Beatty (1875–1968), a Canadian mining millionaire, assembled one of the most significant collections of Islamic and Far Eastern art in the Western world, he donated these to Ireland. Housed in the gorgeous clock tower building of **Dublin Castle**, it's one of Dublin's real hidden gems. Among the library's exhibits are clay tablets from Babylon dating from 2700 BC, Japanese color woodblock prints, Chinese jade books, and Turkish and Persian paintings. The second floor, dedicated to the great religions, houses 250 manuscripts of the Koran from across the Muslim world, as well as one of the earliest gospels. Life-size Buddhas from Burma and rhino cups from China are among the other curios on show. Guided tours of the library are available on Tuesday and Saturday at 2:30 PM. On sunny days you'll find the garden is one of the most tranquil places in central Dublin. *Castle St., Dublin West, tel. 01/407–0750, www.cbl.ie. Free. May–Oct., Mon.–Fri. 10–5, Sat. 11–5, Sun. 1–5; Nov.–Apr., Tues.–Fri. 10–5, Sat. 11–5, Sun. 1–5.*

㊲ ㊼ **THE CHIMNEY.** Just in front of the Chief O'Neill hotel you'll see one of the original brick chimneys of the Old Jameson Distillery, which has been turned into into a 185-ft observation tower with the first 360-degree view of Dublin. Built in 1895, the redbrick chimney now has a two-tiered, glass-enclosed platform at the top. The ride up in the glass elevator is just as thrilling as the view. *Smithfield Village, Dublin West, tel. 01/817–3820, www.chiefoneills.com. €6.35. Mon.–Sat. 10–5:30, Sun. 11–5:30.*

# dublin west

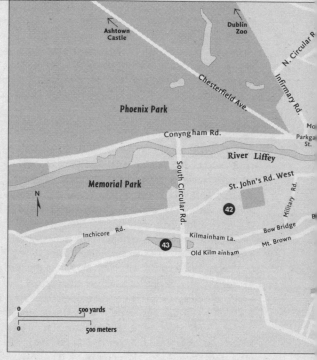

Chester Beatty
Library, 36
The Chimney, 47
Christ Church
Cathedral, 37
City Hall, 34
Dublin Castle, 35
Dublinia, 38

Four Courts, 44
Guinness
Brewery and
Storehouse, 41
Iveagh Market
Hall, 49
Kilmainham
Gaol, 43

Marsh's
Library, 40
National College
of Art
and Design, 50
Old Jameson
Distillery, 46
Royal Hospital
Kilmainham, 42

St. Michan's
Church, 45
St. Nicholas of
Myra's Church, 48
St. Patrick's
Cathedral, 39

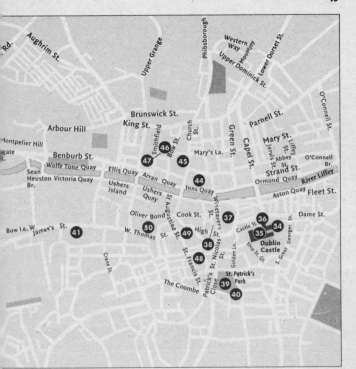

★ **③⑦ CHRIST CHURCH CATHEDRAL.** You'd never know from the outside that the first Christianized Danish king built a wooden church at this site in 1038; thanks to the extensive 19th-century renovation of its stonework and trim, the cathedral looks more Victorian than Anglo-Norman. Construction on the present Christ Church—the flagship of the Church of Ireland and one of two Protestant cathedrals in Dublin (the other is St. Patrick's just to the south)— was begun in 1172 by Strongbow, a Norman baron and conqueror of Dublin for the English crown, and went on for 50 years. By 1875 the cathedral had deteriorated badly; a major renovation gave it much of the look it has today, including the addition of one of Dublin's most charming structures: a Bridge of Sighs–like affair that connects the cathedral to the old Synod Hall, which now holds the Viking extravaganza, Dublinia. Remains from the 12th-century building include the north wall of the nave, the west bay of the choir, and the fine stonework of the transepts, with their pointed arches and supporting columns. Strongbow himself is buried in the cathedral beneath an impressive effigy. The vast, sturdy **crypt,** with its 12th- and 13th-century vaults, is Dublin's oldest surviving structure and the building's most notable feature. At 6 PM on Wednesday and Thursday you can enjoy the glories of a choral evensong. *Christ Church Pl. and Winetavern St., Dublin West, tel. 01/677–8099, www.cccdub.ie.* €2.55. *Daily 9:45–5.*

**③④ CITY HALL.** Facing the Liffey from Cork Hill at the top of Parliament Street, this grand Georgian municipal building (1769–79), once the Royal Exchange, marks the southwestern corner of Temple Bar. Today it's the seat of the Dublin Corporation, the elected body that governs the city. Thomas Cooley designed the building with 12 columns that encircle the domed central rotunda, which has a fine mosaic floor and 12 frescoes depicting Dublin legends and ancient Irish historical scenes. The 20-ft-high sculpture to the right is the "Liberator" Daniel O'Connell. He looks like he's about to begin the famous speech he gave here in 1800. The building houses a multimedia exhibition—with artifacts, kiosks, graphics, and A/V presentations— tracing the evolution of Ireland's 1,000-year-old capital. *Dame St.,*

*Dublin West, tel. 01/672–2204, www.dublincity.ie/cityhall/home.htm.
€3.80. Mon.–Sat. 10–5:15, Sun. 2–5.*

**35 DUBLIN CASTLE.** Neil Jordan's film *Michael Collins* captured Dublin Castle's near indomitable status well: seat and symbol of the British rule of Ireland for 7½ centuries, the castle figured largely in Ireland's turbulent history early in the 20th century. It's now, however, mainly used for Irish and EU governmental purposes. The sprawling **Great Courtyard** is the reputed site of the Black Pool (Dubh Linn, pronounced *dove*-lin) from which Dublin got its name. In the Lower Castle Yard, the **Record Tower,** the earliest of several towers on the site, is the largest remaining relic of the original Norman buildings, built by King John between 1208 and 1220. The clock tower building now houses the **Chester Beatty Library.** Guided tours are available around the principal **State Apartments** (on the southern side of the Upper Castle Yard), formerly the residence of the English viceroys. Now used by the president of Ireland to host visiting heads of state and EU ministers, the State Apartments are lavishly furnished with rich Donegal carpets and illuminated by Waterford glass chandeliers. The largest and most impressive of these chambers, **St. Patrick's Hall,** with its gilt pillars and painted ceiling, is used for the inauguration of Irish presidents. The **Round Drawing Room,** in Bermingham Tower, dates from 1411 and was rebuilt in 1777; a number of Irish leaders were imprisoned in the tower, from the 16th century to the early 20th century. The blue oval **Wedgwood Room** contains Chippendale chairs and a marble fireplace. The **Castle Vaults** now holds an elegant little patisserie and bistro.

Carved oak panels and stained glass depicting viceroys' coats of arms grace the interior of the **Church of the Holy Trinity** (formerly called Chapel Royal), on the castle grounds. The church was designed in 1814 by Francis Johnston, who also designed the original General Post Office building on O'Connell Street. Once you're inside, look up—you'll see an elaborate array of fan vaults on the ceiling. Make sure you also see the more than 100 carved heads that adorn the walls outside. St. Peter and Jonathan Swift preside over the north door, St. Patrick and Brian Boru over the east. One-hour guided tours of the castle are available every half hour, but the rooms are closed when in official use, so phone first. The church is on the castle grounds; the easiest way into the castle is through the **Cork Hill Gate,** just west of City Hall. *Castle St., Dublin West, tel. 01/677–7129, www.dublincastle.ie. State Apartments €4, including tour. Weekdays 10–5, weekends 2–5.*

**③⑧ DUBLINIA.** Dublin's Medieval Trust has set up an entertaining and informative reconstruction of everyday life in medieval Dublin. The main exhibits use high-tech audiovisual and computer displays; there's also a scale model of what Dublin was like around 1500, a medieval maze, a life-size reconstruction based on the 13th-century dockside at Wood Quay, and a fine view from the tower. For a more modern take on the city, check out the James Malton series of prints of 18th-century Dublin, hanging on the walls of the coffee shop. Dublinia is in the old Synod Hall (formerly a meeting place for bishops of the Church of Ireland), attached via a covered stonework Victorian bridge to Christ Church Cathedral. *St. Michael's Hill, Dublin West, tel. 01/679–4611, www.dublinia.ie. Exhibit €5. Apr.–Sept., daily 10–5; Oct.–Mar., Mon.–Sat. 11–4, Sun. 10–4:30.*

**④④ FOUR COURTS.** The stately Corinthian portico and the circular central hall warrant a visit here, to the seat of the High Court of Justice of Ireland. The distinctive copper-covered dome on a colonnaded rotunda makes this one of Dublin's most instantly recognizable buildings; the view from the rotunda is terrific. Built between 1786 and 1802, the Four Courts are James Gandon's second Dublin masterpiece—close on the heels of his **Custom House,** downstream on the same side of the River Liffey. In 1922, during the Irish Civil War, the Four Courts was almost totally destroyed by shelling—the adjoining Public Records Office was gutted, and many priceless legal documents, including innumerable family records, destroyed. Restorations took 10 years. There is no tour of the building, but you are welcome to sit in while the courts are in session. *Inns Quay, Dublin West, tel. 01/872–5555, www.courts.ie. Daily 10–1 and 2:15–4.*

★ **41** **GUINNESS BREWERY AND STOREHOUSE.** Founded by Arthur Guinness in 1759, Ireland's all-dominating brewer—at one time the largest stout-producing brewery in the world—spans a 60-acre spread west of Christ Church Cathedral. Not surprisingly, it's the most popular tourist destination in town—after all, the Irish national drink is Guinness stout, a dark brew made with roasted malt. The brewery itself is closed to the public, but the **Guinness Storehouse** is a spectacular attraction, designed to woo you with the wonders of the "dark stuff." Located in a 1904, cast-iron—and—brick warehouse, the museum display covers six floors built around a huge central glass atrium. Beneath the glass floor of the lobby you'll see Arthur Guinness's original lease on the site, for a whopping 9,000 years. The exhibition elucidates the brewing process and its history, with antique presses and vats, a look at bottle and can design through the ages, a history of the Guinness family, and a fascinating archive of Guinness advertisements. You might think it's all a bit much (it's only a drink, after all), and parts of the exhibit do feel a little over-the-top. The star attraction is undoubtedly the top-floor **Gravity Bar,** with 360-degree floor-to-ceiling glass walls that offer a nonpareil view out over the city at sunset while you sip your free pint. One of the bar's first clients was one William Jefferson Clinton. *St. James' Gate, Dublin West, tel. 01/408–4800, www.guinness.com. €12. Daily 9:30–5.*

**43** **KILMAINHAM GAOL.** Leaders of the 1916 Easter Uprising, including Pádrig Pearse and James Connolly, were held in this grim, forbidding structure before being executed in the prison yard. Other famous inmates included the revolutionary Robert Emmet and Charles Stewart Parnell, a leading politician. You can visit the cells, a chilling sight, while the guided tour and a 30-minute audiovisual presentation relate a graphic account of Ireland's political history over the past 200 years—from a Nationalist viewpoint. You can only visit the prison as part of a guided tour, which leaves every hour on the hour. You'll find a small tearoom on the premises. *Inchicore Rd., Dublin West, tel.* 01/453–5984, *www.heritageireland.ie.* €4.40. *Mon.–Sat.* 9:30–5, *Sun.* 10–5.

**40** **MARSH'S LIBRARY.** When Ireland's first public library was founded and endowed in 1701 by Narcissus Marsh, the Archbishop of Dublin, it was open to "All Graduates and Gentlemen." The two-story brick Georgian building has been practically unchanged inside since then. It houses a priceless collection of 250 manuscripts and 25,000 15th- to 18th-century books. Many of these rare volumes are locked inside cages, as are the readers who wish to peruse them. The cages were to discourage students who, often impecunious, may have been tempted to make the books their own. The library has been restored with great attention to its original architectural details, especially in the book stacks. The library is a short walk west from St. Stephen's Green and accessed through a charming little cottage garden. *St. Patrick's Close off Patrick St., Dublin West, tel.* 01/454–3511, *www.kst.dit.ie/marsh.* €2.50. *Mon. and Wed.–Fri.* 10–12:45 *and* 2–5, *Sat.* 10:30–12:45.

**46** **OLD JAMESON DISTILLERY.** Founded in 1791, this distillery produced one of Ireland's most famous whiskeys for nearly 200 years, until 1966 (at that point, local distilleries merged to form Irish Distillers and moved to a purpose-built, ultramodern distillery in Middleton, County Cork). Part of the complex was converted into the group's head office, and the distillery itself became a museum. There's a short audiovisual history of the industry, which had its origins 1,500 years ago in Middle Eastern perfume making. You can also tour the old distillery, and learn about the distilling of whiskey from grain to bottle, or view a reconstruction of a former warehouse, where the colorful nicknames of former barrel makers are recorded. There's a 20-minute audiovisual show about the making of whiskey at Jameson's distillery, a 40-minute tour, and a complimentary tasting (remember: Irish whiskey is best drunk without a mixer—try it straight or with water); four attendees are invited to taste different brands of Irish whiskey and compare them against bourbon and Scotch. If you have a large group and everyone wants to do this, phone in advance to arrange it. *Bow St., Dublin West, tel. 01/807–2355, www.irish-whiskey-trail.com. €6.50. Daily 9–5:30; tours every ½ hr.*

★ ㊷ **ROYAL HOSPITAL KILMAINHAM.** This replica of Les Invalides in Paris is regarded as the most important 17th-century building in Ireland. Commissioned as a hospice for disabled and veteran soldiers by James Butler—the Duke of Ormonde and Viceroy to King Charles II—the building was completed in 1684, making it the first building built in Dublin's golden age. It survived into the 1920s as a hospital, but after the founding of the Irish Free State in 1922, the building fell into disrepair. Over the last 15 years or so, the entire edifice has been restored to what it once was.

The structure's four galleries are arranged around a courtyard; there's also a grand dining hall—100 ft long by 50 ft wide. The architectural highlight is the hospital's Baroque **chapel,** distinguished by its extraordinary plasterwork ceiling and fine wood carvings. "There is nothing in Ireland from the 17th century that can come near this masterpiece," raved cultural historian John FitzMaurice Mills. The Royal Hospital also houses the **Irish Museum of Modern Art.** The museum displays works by non-Irish, 20th-century greats, including Picasso and Miró, and regularly hosts touring shows from major European museums. They do concentrate, however, on the work of Irish artists: Richard Deacon, Richard Gorman, Dorothy Cross, Sean Scully, Matt Mullican, Louis Le Brocquy, and James Colman are among the contemporary artists represented. The Café Musée has soups, sandwiches, etc. The hospital is a short ride by taxi or bus from the city center. *Kilmainham La., Dublin West, tel. 01/612–9900, www.modernart.ie. Royal Hospital free; individual shows may have separate charges; Museum of Modern Art permanent collection free, small charge for special exhibitions. Royal Hospital Tues.–Sat. 10–*

5:30, Sun. noon–5:30, tours every ½ hr; Museum of Modern Art Tues.–Sat. 10–5:30, Sun. noon–5:30; tours Wed. and Fri. at 2:30, Sat. at 11:30.

**45 ST. MICHAN'S CHURCH.** However macabre, St. Michan's main claim to fame is down in the vaults, where the totally dry atmosphere has preserved a number of corpses in a remarkable state of mummification. They lie in open caskets. Most of the preserved bodies are thought to have been Dublin tradespeople (one was, they say, a religious crusader). Except for its 120-ft-high bell tower, this Anglican church is architecturally undistinguished. The church was built in 1685 on the site of an 11th-century Danish church (Michan was a cannonized Danish saint). Another reason to come is to see the 18th-century organ, which Handel supposedly played for his first performance of the *Messiah*. Don't forget to check out the Stool of Repentance—the only one still in existence in the city. Parishioners judged to be "open and notoriously naughty livers" used it to do public penance. *Lower Church St., Dublin West,* tel. 01/872–4154. €2.55. Apr.–Oct., weekdays 10–12:45 and 2–4:45, Sat. 10–12:45, Sun. service at 10 AM; Nov.–Mar., weekdays 12:30–3:30, Sat. 10–12:45, Sun. service at 10 AM.

**39 ST. PATRICK'S CATHEDRAL.** The largest cathedral in Dublin and also the national cathedral of the Church of Ireland, St. Patrick's is the second of the capital's two Protestant cathedrals. (The other is Christ Church, and the reason Dublin has two cathedrals is because St. Patrick's originally stood outside the walls of Dublin, while its close neighbor was within the walls and belonged to the see of Dublin.) Legend has it that in the 5th century St. Patrick baptized many converts at a well on the site of the cathedral. The original building, dedicated in 1192 and early English Gothic in style, was an unsuccessful attempt to assert supremacy over Christ Church Cathedral. At 305 ft, it's the longest church in the country, a fact Oliver Cromwell's troops—no friends to the Irish— found useful as they made the church's nave into their stable, in the 17th century. They left the building in a terrible state; its current condition is largely due to the benevolence of Sir Benjamin

Guinness—of the brewing family—who started financing major restoration work in 1860.

Make sure you see the gloriously heraldic **Choir of St. Patrick's,** hung with colorful medieval banners, and find the tomb of the most famous of St. Patrick's many illustrious deans, Jonathan Swift, immortal author of *Gulliver's Travels,* who held office from 1713 to 1745. **Swift's tomb** is in the south aisle, not far from that of his beloved "Stella," Mrs. Esther Johnson. Swift's epitaph is inscribed over the robing-room door. Yeats—who translated it thus: "Swift has sailed into his rest; Savage indignation there cannot lacerate his breast"—declared it the greatest epitaph of all time. Other memorials include the 17th-century **Boyle Monument,** with its numerous painted figures of family members, and the **monument to Turlough O'Carolan,** the last of the Irish bards and one of the country's finest harp players. Immediately north of the cathedral is a small park, with statues of many of Dublin's literary figures and **St. Patrick's Well.** "Living Stones" is the cathedral's permanent exhibition celebrating St. Patrick's place in the life of the city. If you're a music lover, you're in for a treat; matins (9:45 AM) and evensong (5:35 PM) are still sung on most days. *Patrick St., Dublin West, tel. 01/453–9472, www.stpatrickscathedral.ie. €3.45. May and Sept.– Oct., weekdays 9–6, Sat. 9–5, Sun. 10–11 and 12:45–3; June–Aug., weekdays 9–6, Sat. 9–4, Sun. 9:30–3 and 4:15–5:15; Nov.–Apr., weekdays 9–6, Sat. 9–4, Sun. 10–11 and 12:45–3.*

## THE LIBERTIES

A stroll through the Liberties puts you in square working-class Dublin, past and present, good and bad. The name derives from Dublin of the Middle Ages, when the area south and west of Christ Church Cathedral was outside the city walls and free from the jurisdiction of the city rulers. A certain amount of freedom, or "liberty," was enjoyed by those who settled here, which attracted people on the fringes of society, especially the poor.

## A Good Walk

*Numbers in the text correspond to numbers in the margin and on the Dublin West map.*

Start on Patrick Street, in the shadow of St. Patrick's Cathedral. Look down the street toward the Liffey and take in the glorious view of Christ Church. Go right on Dean Street, where you'll find John Fallons pub. Take a right off Dean Street onto Francis Street and walk uphill. A number of quality antiques shops line both sides of the thoroughfare. Halfway up Francis Street, on the right, behind hefty wrought-iron gates, you'll discover one of Dublin's most-overlooked treasures: **ST. NICHOLAS OF MYRA'S CHURCH** ㊽. Continue up Francis Street and take the next right onto Thomas Davis Street (named after a famous patriot and revolutionary—the Liberties has long had a close association with Irish Nationalism). The street is full of classic, two-story redbrick houses. The area, once the heart of "Darlin' Dublin" and the holy source of its distinctive accent, is rapidly becoming yuppified. Back on Francis Street, in an old factory building with its chimney stack intact, you'll find an exciting market, **IVEAGH MARKET HALL** ㊾. At the top of Francis Street turn left onto Thomas Street. Across the road, on your right side, stands the wonderfully detailed exterior of St. Augustine and St. John, with its grandiose spire stretching above it. You'll notice churches all over the Liberties; the bishops thought it wise to build holy palaces in the poorest areas of the city as tall, shining beacons of comfort and hope. Farther up Thomas Street in another converted factory is the **NATIONAL COLLEGE OF ART AND DESIGN** ㊿.

### TIMING

Unless you intend on doing some serious antiques shopping, this is a relatively quick stroll—perhaps two hours—as the Liberties is a compact area of small, winding streets.

## What to See

(49) **IVEAGH MARKET HALL.** One of numerous buildings bestowed upon the city of Dublin by Lord Iveagh of the Guinness family, the cavernous, Victorian, redbrick-and-granite Iveagh Market Hall holds an eclectic market—with books, vintage clothes, records, and jewelry—from Tuesday to Saturday. *Francis St., Dublin West. Free. Tues.–Sat. 9–5.*

(50) **NATIONAL COLLEGE OF ART AND DESIGN.** The delicate welding of glass and iron onto the redbrick Victorian facade of this onetime factory makes this school worth a visit. Walk around the cobblestone central courtyard, where there's always the added bonus of viewing some of the students working away in glass, clay, metal, and stone. *Thomas St., Dublin West, tel. 01/671–1377, www.ncad.ie. Free. Weekdays 9–7.*

(48) **ST. NICHOLAS OF MYRA'S CHURCH.** A grand Neoclassical style characterizes this church, completed in 1834. The highly ornate chapel inside includes ceiling panels of the 12 apostles, and a pietà raised 20 ft above the marble altar, guarded on each side by angels sculpted by John Hogan while he was in Florence. The tiny nuptial chapel to the right has a small Harry Clarke stained-glass window. *St. Nicholas St., Dublin West. Free. Hrs vary.*

## NORTH OF THE LIFFEY

If you stand on O'Connell Bridge or the pedestrian-only Ha'penny span, you'll get excellent views up and down the Liffey, in Gaelic known as the *abha na life*, which James Joyce transcribed phonetically as Anna Livia in *Finnegan's Wake*. Here, framed with embankments just like those along Paris's Seine, the river nears the end of its 128-km (80-mi) journey from the Wicklow Mountains into the Irish Sea. And near the the bridges, you begin a pilgrimage into James Joyce Country—north of the Liffey, in the center of town—and the captivating sights of Dublin's northside, a mix of densely thronged shopping streets and recently refurbished genteel homes.

The northside *absolutely* warrants a walk, for three reasons: major cultural institutions (the Gate Theatre, the James Joyce Cultural Centre, the Dublin Writers Museum, and the Hugh Lane Municipal Gallery of Modern Art), sites of historical significance with ties to Irish Republicanism, and vibrant, busy streets.

During the 18th century, most of the upper echelons of Dublin society lived in the Georgian houses in the northside—around Mountjoy Square—and shopped along Capel Street, which was lined with stores selling fine furniture and silver. But southside development—Merrion Square in 1764, the Georgian Leinster House in 1745, and Fitzwilliam Square in 1825—permanently changed the northside's fortunes. The city's fashionable social center crossed the Liffey, and although some of the northside's illustrious inhabitants stuck it out, this area gradually became more run-down. The northside's fortunes have changed, however. Once-derelict swaths of houses, especially on and near the Liffey, have been rehabilitated, and large new shopping centers have opened on Mary and Jervis streets. A huge shopping mall and entertainment complex are planned for O'Connell Street, right where the defunct Carlton Cinema stands. Precisely because the exciting redevelopment that transformed Temple Bar is still in its early stages here—*because* it's a place on the cusp of transition—the northside is an intriguing part of town to visit.

## A Good Walk

*Numbers in the text correspond to numbers in the margin and on the Dublin City Center map.*

Begin at O'Connell Bridge—if you look closely at it you will notice that it is wider than it is long—and head north up **O'CONNELL STREET** ⑤②. Stop to admire the monument to Daniel O'Connell, "The Liberator," erected as a tribute to the great orator's achievement in securing Catholic Emancipation in 1829 (note the obvious scars from the fighting of 1916 on the figures). A quick trip down middle Abbey Street takes you to the brand-new **HOT PRESS IRISH MUSIC HALL OF FAME** ⑤, a museum dedicated to Irish pop music. Then continue north to the **GENERAL POST OFFICE** ㊾, a major site in the Easter Uprising of 1916. O'Connell leads to the southeastern corner of Parnell Square. Heading counterclockwise around the square, you'll pass in turn the **GATE THEATRE** ㊿ and **ABBEY PRESBYTERIAN CHURCH** ㊿ before coming to the **DUBLIN WRITERS MUSEUM** ㊿ and the **HUGH LANE MUNICIPAL GALLERY OF MODERN ART** ㊿, both on the north side of the square and both housed in glorious neoclassic mansions; these are the two sites where you should plan to spend most of your time on the northside. Either before you go in or after you come out, you might also want to visit the solemn yet serene **GARDEN OF REMEMBRANCE** ㊿.

From here, you have two choices: to continue exploring the cultural sights that lie to the northeast of Parnell Square and east of O'Connell Street or to head to Moore, Henry, and Mary streets for a flavor of middle-class Dublin that you won't get on the spiffier southside. If you decide to continue your cultural explorations, jump two blocks northeast of Parnell Square to the **JAMES JOYCE CULTURAL CENTRE** ㊿, and then head farther northeast to the once glamorous **MOUNTJOY SQUARE** ㉖. Half a mile east of Mountjoy Square is Croke Park, gaelic football stadium and home to the Gaelic Athletic Association's **GAA MUSEUM** ㉒. Return to Mountjoy Square and turn south, stopping in at the **ST. FRANCIS XAVIER CHURCH** ㉑ on Gardiner Street. Head back west to Marlborough Street (parallel to and between Gardiner and O'Connell streets) to visit the **PRO-CATHEDRAL** ㉓. Continue down to the quays and jog a block east to the **CUSTOM HOUSE** ㉔. If you decide to shop with the locals, leave Parnell Square via the southwestern corner, stopping first to check out the chapel at the **ROTUNDA**

**HOSPITAL** ⑥⑤; Moore Street is your first left off Parnell Street and leads directly to Henry Street.

### TIMING

The northside has fewer major attractions than the southside and, overall, is less picturesque. As a result, you're unlikely to want to stroll as leisurely here. If you zipped right through this walk, you could be done in less than two hours. But the two major cultural institutions—the Dublin Writers Museum and the Hugh Lane Municipal Gallery of Modern Art—easily deserve several hours each, so it's worth doing this walk only if you have the time to devote to them. Also, a number of additional sights connected with James Joyce and *Ulysses*—covered in **"ReJoyce! A Walk through James Joyce's Dublin and Ulysses"**—are in the vicinity, so if you're a devoted Joycean, consult the Close-Up box before setting out on this walk.

## What to See

⑤⑤ **ABBEY PRESBYTERIAN CHURCH.** A soaring spire marks the exterior of this church, popularly known as Findlater's Church—after Alex Findlater, a noted Dublin grocer who endowed it. Completed in 1864, the church stands on the northeast corner of Parnell Square; the inside has a stark Presbyterian mood, despite stained-glass windows and ornate pews. For a bird's-eye view, take the small staircase that leads to the balcony. *Parnell Sq., North of the Liffey, tel. 01/837–8600. Free. Hrs vary.*

⑥④ **CUSTOM HOUSE.** Seen at its best reflected in the waters of the Liffey during the short interval when the high tide is on the turn, the Custom House is the city's most spectacular Georgian building. Extending 375 ft on the north side of the river, this is the work of James Gandon, an English architect who arrived in Ireland in 1781, when construction commenced (it continued for 10 years). Crafted from gleaming Portland stone, the central portico is linked by arcades to the pavilions at either end. Unfortunately, the dome is on the puny side and out of proportion. A statue of

Commerce tops the copper dome; statues on the main facade are based on allegorical themes. Note the exquisitely carved lions and unicorns supporting the arms of Ireland at the far ends of the facade. Republicans set the building on fire in 1921, but it was completely restored and now houses government offices. The building opened to the public in mid-1997 after having been closed for many years, and with it came a new visitor center tracing the building's history and significance, and the life of Gandon. *Custom House Quay, North of the Liffey, tel. 01/878–7660. €1.27. Mid-Mar.–Oct., weekdays 10–5:30, weekends 2–5:30; Nov.–Feb., Wed.–Fri. 10–5, Sun. 2–5:30.*

★ ⑤⑥ **DUBLIN WRITERS MUSEUM.** "If you would know Ireland—body and soul—you must read its poems and stories," wrote Yeats in 1891. Further investigation into the Irish way with words can be found here at this unique museum, in a magnificently restored 18th-century town house on the north side of Parnell Square. Once the home of John Jameson (of the Irish whiskey family), the mansion centers on an enormous drawing room, gorgeously decorated with paintings, Adamesque plasterwork, and a deep Edwardian lincrusta frieze. Rare manuscripts, diaries, posters, letters, limited and first editions, photographs, and other mementoes commemorate the life and works of the nation's greatest writers (and there are many of them, so leave plenty of time), including Joyce, Shaw, J. M. Synge, Lady Gregory, Yeats, Beckett, and many others. On display are an 1804 edition of Swift's *Gulliver's Travels*, an 1899 first edition of Bram Stoker's *Dracula*, and an 1899 edition of Wilde's *Ballad of Reading Gaol*. There's even a special "Teller of Tales" exhibit showcasing Behan, O'Flaherty, and O'Faolan. Readings are periodically held. The bookshop and café make this an ideal place to spend a rainy afternoon. If you lose track of time and stay until the closing hour, you might want to dine at Chapter One, a highly regarded restaurant in the basement, which would have had Joyce ecstasizing about its currant-sprinkled scones. *18 Parnell Sq. N, North of the Liffey, tel. 01/872–2077, www.visitdublin.com. €5.50. June–*

Aug., Mon.–Fri. 10–6, Sat. 10–5, Sun. 11–5; Sept.–May, Mon.–Sat. 10–5, Sun. 11–5.

**62 GAA MUSEUM.** In the bowels of Croke Park, the main stadium and headquarters of the GAA (Gaelic Athletics Association), this museum gives you a great introduction to native Irish sport. The four Gaelic games (football, hurling, camogie, and handball) are explained in detail, and if you're brave enough you can have a go yourself. High-tech displays take you through the history and highlights of the games. *National Awakening* is a really smart, interesting short film reflecting the key impact of the GAA on the emergence of the Irish Nation and the forging of a new Irish identity. The exhilarating *A Day in September* captures the thrill and passion of All Ireland finals day—the annual denouement of the inter-county hurling and Gaelic football—every bit as important to the locals as the Superbowl is in the US. *New Stand, Croke Park, North County Dublin, tel. 01/855–8176, www.gaa.ie; €5.00; May–Sept., daily 9:30–5; Oct.–Apr., Tues.–Sat. 10–5, Sun. noon–5.*

**58 GARDEN OF REMEMBRANCE.** Opened in 1966, 50 years after the Easter Uprising of 1916, the garden in Parnell Square commemorates those who died fighting for Ireland's freedom. At the garden's entrance you'll find a large plaza; steps lead down to the fountain area, graced with a sculpture by contemporary Irish artist Oisín Kelly, based on the mythological Children of Lír, who were turned into swans. The garden serves as an oasis of tranquillity in the middle of the busy city. *Parnell Sq., North of the Liffey. Daily 9–5.*

**54 GATE THEATRE.** The Gate has been one of Dublin's most important theaters since its founding in 1929 by Micháel MacLiammóir and Hilton Edwards (who also founded Galway City's An Taibhdhearc as the national Irish-language theater). The theatre stages many innovative productions by Irish playwrights, as well as by foreign playwrights—and plenty of foreign actors have performed here, including Orson Welles (his first paid performance) and James Mason (early in his career). Shows here begin as soon as you walk into the auditorium—a Georgian masterwork designed by Richard Johnston in 1784 as an assembly room for the Rotunda Hospital complex. Today the theater plays it safe with a major repertory of European and North American drama and new plays by established Irish writers. *Cavendish Row, North of the Liffey, tel. 01/ 874–4045. Shows Mon.–Sat.*

**53** **GENERAL POST OFFICE.** Known as the GPO, it is one of the great civic buildings of Dublin's Georgian era, but it's famous because of the role it played in the Easter Uprising. It has an impressive facade in the neoclassical style, and was designed by Francis Johnston and built by the British between 1814 and 1818 as a center of communications. This gave it great strategic importance—and was one of the reasons why it was chosen by the insurgent forces in 1916 as a headquarters. Here, on Easter Monday, 1916, the Republican forces, about 2,000 in number and under the guidance of Pádrig Pearse and James Connolly, stormed the building and issued the Proclamation of the Irish Republic. After a week of shelling, the GPO lay in ruins; 13 rebels were ultimately executed (including Connolly, who was dying of gangrene from a leg shattered in the fighting and had to be propped up in a chair before the firing squad). Most of the original building was destroyed, though the facade survived (you can still see the scars of bullets on its pillars). Rebuilt and subsequently reopened in 1929, it became a working post office—with an attractive two-story main concourse. A bronze sculpture depicting the dying Cuchulainn, a leader of the Red Branch Knights in Celtic mythology, sits in the front window. The 1916 Proclamation and the names of its signatories are inscribed on the green marble plinth. *O'Connell St., North of the Liffey, tel. 01/872–8888, www.anpost.ie. Free. Mon.–Sat. 8–8, Sun. 10:30–6.*

**51** **HOT PRESS IRISH MUSIC HALL OF FAME.** A few years ago Ireland's flagship music magazine had the clever idea of opening a museum dedicated to Irish rock and pop music. Ireland has had a large impact on the world music scene, and the Hall of Fame is like a garage sale for the greats of Irish pop music: Van Morrison's big hat, Bob Geldof's cheap guitar, Sinéad O'Connor's self-mutilated jeans, the Corrs' infinitesimally small dresses, and, of course, Bono's superfly Zooropa shoes—all neatly piled in chronological order. The self-guided audio tour takes you through the highs and lows of this musical journey, from the Beat bands of the '60s; '70s punk bands with rockin' names like Stiff Little Fingers; the 1980s, when U2 was the world's most popular band; through to the boy bands and diva-driven (Sinéad, Andrea Corr, Delores O'Riordian of the Cranberries) '90s scene. Favorite items include Sinéad O'Connor's first royalty check from Island records for £13.66. It's uncashed. *57 Middle Abbey St., North of the Liffey, tel. 01/878–3345, www.imhf.com. €5.70. Apr.–Sept., daily 10–6; Oct.–Mar., daily 11–5.*

★ ❺⃝ **HUGH LANE MUNICIPAL GALLERY OF MODERN ART.** Built originally as a town house for the Earl of Charlemont in 1762, this residence was so grand its Parnell Square street was nicknamed "Palace Row" in its honor. Designed by Sir William Chambers (who also built the Marino Casino for Charlemont) in the best Palladian manner, its delicate and rigidly correct facade, extended by two demilune arcades, was fashioned from the "new" white Ardmulcan stone (now seasoned to gray). Charlemont was one of the cultural locomotives of 18th-century Dublin—his walls were hung with Titians and Hogarths, and he frequently dined with Oliver Goldsmith and Sir Joshua Reynolds—so he would undoubtedly be delighted that his home is now the Hugh Lane Gallery, named after a nephew of Lady Gregory (Yeats's aristocratic patron). Lane collected both Impressionist paintings and 19th-century Irish and Anglo-Irish works. A complicated agreement with the National Gallery in London (reached after heated diplomatic dispute) stipulates that a portion of the 39 French paintings amassed by Lane shuttle back and forth between London and here. You can see Pissarro's *Printemps*, Manet's *Eva Gonzales*, Morisot's *Jour d'Été*, and, the jewel of the collection, Renoir's *Les Parapluies*.

In something of a snub to the British art establishment, the late Francis Bacon's partner donated the entire contents of the artist's studio to the Hugh Lane Gallery. The studio of Britain's arguably premier 20th-century artist has been reconstructed in all its gaudy glory in Dublin. It gives you, however, a unique opportunity: to observe the working methods of the artist responsible for such masterpieces as *Study After Velázquez 1950* and the tragic splash-and-crash *Triptych*. The reconstructed studio will remain on permanent display, along with Bacon's diary (that should be worth a read), books, and anything else they picked up off his floor.

Between the collection of Irish paintings in the **National Gallery of Ireland** and the superlative works on view here, you can quickly become familiar with Irish 20th-century art. Irish artists represented include Roderic O'Conor, well known for his views of the West of Ireland; William Leech, including his *Girl with a Tinsel Scarf* (ca. 1912) and *The Cigarette*; and the most famous of the group, Jack B. Yeats (W. B.'s brother). The museum has a dozen of his paintings, including *Ball Alley* (ca. 1927) and *There Is No Night* (1949). There is also strikingly displayed stained-glass work by early 20th-century Irish master artisans Harry Clarke and Evie Hone. *Parnell Sq. N, North of the Liffey, tel. 01/874–1903, www.hughlane.ie. Free (Bacon Studio €7.50). Tues.–Thurs. 9:30–6, Fri.–Sat. 9:30–5, Sun. 11–5.*

⑤⑨ **JAMES JOYCE CULTURAL CENTRE.** Everyone in Ireland has at least heard of James Joyce—especially since a copy of his censored and suppressed *Ulysses* was one of the top status symbols of the early 20th century. Joyce is of course now acknowledged as one of the greatest modern authors, and his *Dubliners*, *Finnegan's Wake*, and *A Portrait of the Artist as a Young Man* can even be read as quirky "travel guides" to Dublin. Open to the general public, this restored 18th-century Georgian town house, once the dancing academy of Professor Denis J. Maginni (which many will recognize from *Ulysses*), is a center for Joycean studies and events related to the author. It has an extensive library and archives, exhibition rooms, a bookstore, and a café. The collection includes letters from Beckett, Joyce's guitar and cane, and a celebrated edition of *Ulysses* illustrated by Matisse. Along with housing the **Joyce Museum** in Sandycove, the center is the main organizer of "Bloomstime," which marks the week leading up to June 16's Bloomsday celebrations. (Bloomsday, June 16, is the single day *Ulysses* chronicles, as Leopold Bloom winds his way around Dublin in 1904.) *35 N. Great George's St., North of the Liffey, tel. 01/878–8547, www.jamesjoyce.ie. €5.50. Apr.–Oct., Mon.–Sat. 10–1 and 2–6, Sun. 2–6; Nov.–Mar. by appointment only.*

**60 MOUNTJOY SQUARE.** Built over the two decades before 1818, this square was once surrounded by elegant, terraced houses. Today only the northern side remains intact. The houses on the once derelict southern side have been converted into apartments. Irishman Brian Boru, who led his soldiers to victory against the Vikings in the Battle of Clontarf in 1014, was said to have pitched camp before the confrontation on the site of Mountjoy Square. Playwright Sean O'Casey once lived here at No. 35 and used the square as a setting for *The Shadow of a Gunman*.

**52 O'CONNELL STREET.** Dublin's most famous thoroughfare, 150 ft wide, was previously known as Sackville Street, but its name was changed in 1924, two years after the founding of the Irish Free State. After the devastation of the 1916 Easter Uprising, the street had to be almost entirely reconstructed, a task that took until the end of the 1920s. The main attraction of the street, **Nelson's Pillar**, a Doric column towering over the city center and a marvelous vantage point, was blown up in 1966, the 50th anniversary of the Easter Uprising. The large **monument** at the south end of the street is dedicated to Daniel O'Connell (1775–1847), "The Liberator," and was erected in 1854 as a tribute to the orator's achievement in securing Catholic Emancipation in 1829. Seated winged figures represent the four Victories—courage, eloquence, fidelity, and patriotism—all exemplified by O'Connell. Ireland's four ancient provinces—Munster, Leinster, Ulster, and Connacht—are identified by their respective coats of arms. Look closely and you'll notice that O'Connell is wearing a glove on one hand, as he did for much of his adult life, a self-imposed penance for shooting a man in a duel. Alongside O'Connell is another noted statue, a modern rendition of Joyce's **Anna Livia**, seen as a lady set within a waterfall and now nicknamed by the natives the "floozy in the Jacuzzi." **O'Connell Bridge,** the main bridge spanning the Liffey (wider than it is long), marks the street's southern end.

---

**NEED A BREAK?** On the northside you'll find a number of good places to take a break. One of Dublin's oldest hotels, the **GRESHAM** (Upper O'Connell St., North of the Liffey, tel. 01/874–6881) is a pleasant, old-fashioned spot for a morning coffee or afternoon tea. **CONWAY'S** (Parnell St. near Upper O'Connell St., North of the Liffey, tel. 01/873–2687), founded in 1745, is reputed to be Dublin's second-oldest pub. It's unpretentious and has great pub-grub. For a real Irish pub lunch, stop in at **JOHN M. KEATING** (14 Mary St., North of the Liffey, tel. 01/873–1567), at the corner of Mary and Jervis streets; head upstairs, where you can sit at a low table and chat with locals.

---

**63 PRO-CATHEDRAL.** Dublin's principal Catholic cathedral (also known as St. Mary's) is a great place to hear the best Irish male voices—a Palestrina choir, in which the great Irish tenor John McCormack began his career, sings in Latin here every Sunday at 11. The cathedral, built between 1816 and 1825, has a classical church design—one that's on a suitably epic scale. The church's facade, with a six-Doric-pillared portico, is based on the Temple of Theseus in Athens; the interior is modeled after the Grecian-Doric style of St-Philippe du Roule in Paris. But the building was never granted full cathedral status, nor has the identity of its architect ever been discovered; the only clue is in the church ledger, which lists a "Mr. P." as the builder. *Marlborough St., North of the Liffey, tel. 01/874–5441, www.procathedral.ie. Free. Daily 8 AM–6 PM.*

**ⓐ ROTUNDA HOSPITAL.** Founded in 1745 as the first maternity hospital in Ireland or Britain, the Rotunda was designed on a grand scale by architect Richard Castle (1690–1751), with a three-story tower and a copper cupola. It's now most worth a visit for its **chapel**, with elaborate plasterwork executed by Bartholomew Cramillion between 1757 and 1758, appropriately honoring motherhood. The **Gate Theatre,** in a lavish Georgian assembly room, is also part of the complex. The public is not allowed inside. *Parnell St., North of the Liffey, tel. 01/873–0700.*

**ⓑ ST. FRANCIS XAVIER CHURCH.** One of the city's finest churches in the classical style, the Jesuit St. Francis Xavier's was begun in 1829, the year of Catholic Emancipation, and was completed three years later. The building is designed in the shape of a Latin cross, with a distinctive Ionic portico and an unusual coffered ceiling. The striking, faux-marble high altarpiece, decorated with lapis lazuli, came from Italy. The church appears in James Joyce's story "Grace." *Upper Gardiner St., North of the Liffey, tel. 01/836–3411. Free. Daily 7 AM–8:30 PM.*

## ALONG THE GRAND CANAL

At its completion in 1795, the 547-km (342-mi) Grand Canal was celebrated as the longest in Britain and Ireland. It connected Dublin to the River Shannon, and horse-drawn barges carried cargo (mainly turf) and passengers to the capital from all over the country. By the mid-19th century the train had arrived and the great waterway slowly fell into decline, until the last commercial traffic ceased in 1960. But the 6-km (4-mi) loop around the capital is ideal for a leisurely stroll.

### A Good Walk

*Numbers in the text correspond to numbers in the margin and on the Dublin City Center map.*

Begin by walking down the Pearse Street side of Trinity College until you arrive at the Ringsend Road Bridge. Raised on stilts above the canal is the **WATERWAYS VISITORS CENTRE** ⑥⑥. Head west along the bank until you reach the **MOUNT STREET BRIDGE** ⑥⑦. On the southside is Percy Place, a street with elegant, three-story, terraced houses. On the northside, a small lane leads up to the infamous **SCRUFFY MURPHY'S** ⑥⑧ pub. Taking a little detour at the next right, you'll pass a road that leads up to St. Stephen's. Another right takes you into Powerscourt, a classic, inner-city estate of two-up, two-down terraced houses. Return to the canal and continue your walk along Herbert Place. You can get really close to the dark green water here as it spills over one of the many wood-and-iron locks (all still in working order) that service the canal. James Joyce lost his virginity to a prostitute on the next stretch of the Canal, around Lower Baggot Street Bridge, but these banks belong to the lonesome ghost of another writer, Patrick Kavanagh. A life-size **STATUE OF PATRICK KAVANAGH** ⑥⑨ sits here, contemplative, arms folded, legs crossed on a wooden bench. Less than 2 km (1 mi) past Kavanagh's statue the canal narrows as it approaches Richmond Bridge. Just beyond the bridge is the **IRISH JEWISH MUSEUM** ⑦⓪. To finish your walk in style, take a right onto Richmond Street, past a few antiques stores, until you arrive at **BAMBRICK'S** ⑦①, a public house in the best tradition of Dublin.

## TIMING

You could walk this section of the canal in half an hour if you hurried, but a leisurely pace best suits a waterside walk, so give yourself a couple of hours to visit the Jewish Museum and explore the old streets off the canal.

## What to See

⑦① **BAMBRICK'S.** This is a pub in the best Irish tradition: a long, dark-wood bar, half-empty, frequented mostly by men over 50, and with a staff whose sharp, grinning humor verges on rudeness. 11

Richmond St. South, South of the Liffey, tel. 01/475–4402. Free. Daily 11 AM–midnight.

**70 IRISH JEWISH MUSEUM.** Roughly 5,000 European Jews fleeing the pogroms of Eastern Europe arrived in Ireland in the late 19th century and early 20th century. Today the Jewish population hovers around 1,800. The museum, opened in 1985 by Israeli president Chaim Herzog (himself Dublin-educated), includes a restored synagogue and a display of photographs, letters, and personal memorabilia culled from Dublin's most prominent Jewish families. Exhibits trace the Jewish presence in Ireland back to 1067. In homage to Leopold Bloom, the Jewish protagonist of Joyce's *Ulysses*, every Jewish reference in the novel has been identified. The museum is a 20-minute walk or so from St. Stephen's Green. *3–4 Walworth Rd., South of the Liffey, tel. 01/453–1797. Free. Oct.–Apr., Sun. 10:30–2:30; May–Sept., Tues., Thurs., and Sun. 11–3:30; also by appointment.*

**67 MOUNT STREET BRIDGE.** The bridge has a wooden lock on either side and is the perfect spot to watch these original gateways to the canal in operation. On the southwest corner of the bridge a small stone monument commemorates the battle of Mount Street Bridge in 1916 and the Irish Volunteers who died on this spot.

**68 SCRUFFY MURPHY'S.** Many a backroom deal by the country's political power brokers has been made in the back room of this classy wood-and-brass pub. It's the perfect spot for a pint and a snack. *Lower Mount St., South of the Liffey, tel. 01/661–5006. Free. Daily 11 AM–midnight.*

**69 STATUE OF PATRICK KAVANAGH.** Patrick Kavanagh—Ireland's great rural poet who in 1942 published his best-known poem, "The Great Hunger," about farming and poverty—spent the later years of his life sitting on a bench here writing about the canal, which flowed from his birthplace in the Midlands to the city where he would die. In one such poem he tells those who outlive him, "O commemorate me with no hero-courageous tomb, just a canal-bank seat for the passerby." Acknowledging Kavanagh's devotion to this spot, his friends commissioned a life-size bronze of the poet here. *Canal bank along Wilton Terr., South of the Liffey.*

⑥⑥ **WATERWAYS VISITORS CENTRE.** In the airy, wood-and-glass building you can learn about the history of Irish rivers and canals through photos, videos, and models. *Grand Canal Quay, South of the Liffey, tel. 01/677–7501. €2.55. June–Sept., daily 9:30–5:30; Oct.– May, Wed.–Sun. 12:30–5:30.*

## PHOENIX PARK AND ENVIRONS

Far and away Dublin's largest park, Phoenix Park (the name is an anglicization of the Irish *Fionn Uisce,* meaning clear water) is a vast, green arrowhead-shaped oasis north of the Liffey, a 20-or-so-minute walk from the city center. Dubliners flock here to "take it aisy." It remains the city's main lung, escape valve, sports center (cricket, soccer, Gaelic games, and polo), and home to the noble creatures of the Dublin Zoo. A handful of other cultural sites near the park are also worth visiting, but to combine a visit to any of them with any of our other walks would be a bit difficult. Smithfield and the Old Jameson Distillery, at the end of the Dublin West walk, are the sites closest (the Guinness Brewery and Storehouse, across the river, is also fairly close). So if you do make it to any of those, think about whether you have enough time to append a visit to one or another of these sites. Otherwise, plan to make a special trip out here— walk if you're up to it, or take a car or cab.

### A Good Walk

*Numbers in the text correspond to numbers in the margin and on the Dublin West map.*

Beginning at the Custom House, walk down the quays on the north side of the Liffey until you come to Blackhall Place. Walk up to Arbour Hill and turn left: the **ARBOUR HILL CEMETERY** will be on your left. Directly across Arbour Hill are the **COLLINS BARRACKS**, now a branch of the National Museum (the main entrance is on Benburb Street on the south side). On its east side Benburb becomes Parkgate Street, and it's just a short stroll farther down to the main entrance of **PHOENIX PARK**.

## TIMING

Phoenix Park is *big*; exploring it on foot could easily take the better part of a day. If you're looking for a little exercise, head here: jogging, horseback riding, and bicycling are the ideal ways to explore the park more quickly than you can simply by strolling.

## What to See

**ARBOUR HILL CEMETERY.** All 14 Irishmen executed by the British following the 1916 Easter Uprising are buried here, including Pádrig Pearse, who led the rebellion; his younger brother Willie, who played a minor role in the uprising; and James Connolly, a socialist and labor leader wounded in the battle. Too weak from his wounds to stand, Connolly was tied to a chair and then shot. The burial ground is a simple but formal area, with the names of the dead leaders carved in stone beside an inscription of the proclamation they issued during the uprising. *Arbour Hill, Dublin West. Free. Mon.–Sat. 9–4:30, Sun. 9:30–noon.*

**COLLINS BARRACKS.** The huge Collins Barracks (named for the assassinated Republican leader Michael Collins) houses a section of the National Museum—their collection of glass, silver, furniture, and other decorative arts; exhibitions on Irish military history; and an exhibition of 200 years of Irish costumes and jewelry. A prize exhibit is a 2,000-year-old Japanese ceremonial bell. *Benburb St., Dublin West, tel. 01/677-7444, www.museum.ie. Free. Tues.–Sat. 10–5, Sun. 2–5.*

★ ☾ **PHOENIX PARK.** Europe's largest public park, which extends about 5 km (3 mi) along the Liffey's north bank, encompasses 1,752 acres of verdant green lawns, woods, lakes, and playing fields. It's a jogger's paradise. Sunday is the best time to visit: games of cricket, soccer, polo, baseball, hurling—a combination of lacrosse, baseball, and field hockey—and Irish football are likely to be in progress. Old-fashioned gas lamps line both sides of **Chesterfield Avenue,** the main road that bisects the park for 4 km (2½ mi), which was named for Lord Chesterfield, a lord lieutenant of Ireland, who laid out the road in the 1740s. To the right as you enter the park, you'll see the **People's Garden,** a colorful flower garden designed in 1864.

Among the park's major monuments are the **Phoenix Column,** erected by Lord Chesterfield in 1747, and the **198-ft obelisk,** built in 1817 to commemorate the Duke of Wellington, the Irish general who defeated Napoléon for the British. (Wellington was born in Dublin but, true to the anti-Irish prejudice so prevalent in 19th-century England, balked at the suggestion that he was Irish: "If a man is born in a stable, it doesn't mean he is a horse," he is reputed to have said.) A tall **white cross** marks the spot where Pope John Paul II addressed more than a million people during his 1979 visit to Ireland. Wild deer can be seen grazing in the many open spaces of the park, especially near here.

You're guaranteed to see wildlife at the **Dublin Zoo,** the third-oldest public zoo in the world, founded in 1830, and just a short walk beyond the People's Garden. The place looks a little dilapidated, but the government has allocated money for a five-year renovation that is now under way. Animals from tropical climes are kept in barless enclosures, and Arctic species swim in the lakes close to the reptile house. Interestingly, the zoo is one of the few places in the world where lions will breed in captivity. Some 700 lions have been bred here since the 1850s, one of whom became familiar to movie fans the world over when MGM used him for its trademark. (As they will tell you at the zoo, he is

## Smart Sightseeings

Savvy travelers and others who take their sightseeing seriously have skills worth knowing about.

**DON'T PLAN YOUR VISIT IN YOUR HOTEL ROOM** Don't wait until you pull into town to decide how to spend your days. It's inevitable that there will be much more to see and do than you'll have time for: choose sights in advance.

**ORGANIZE YOUR TOURING** Note the places that most interest you on a map, and visit places that are near each other during the same morning or afternoon.

**START THE DAY WELL EQUIPPED** Leave your hotel in the morning with everything you need for the day—maps, medicines, extra film, your guidebook, rain gear, and another layer of clothing in case the weather turns cooler.

**TOUR MUSEUMS EARLY** If you're there when the doors open you'll have an intimate experience of the collection.

**EASY DOES IT** See museums in the mornings, when you're fresh, and visit sit-down attractions later on. Take breaks before you need them.

**STRIKE UP A CONVERSATION** Only curmudgeons don't respond to a smile and a polite request for information. Most people appreciate your interest in their home town. And your conversations may end up being your most vivid memories.

**GET LOST** When you do, you never know what you'll find—but you can count on it being memorable. Use your guidebook to help you get back on track. Build wandering-around time into every day.

**QUIT BEFORE YOU'RE TIRED** There's no point in seeing that one extra sight if you're too exhausted to enjoy it.

**TAKE YOUR MOTHER'S ADVICE** Go to the bathroom when you have the chance. You never know what lies ahead.

in fact yawning in that familiar shot: an American lion had to be hired to roar and the "voice" was dubbed.) An African Plains area houses the zoo's larger species. The Pets Corner and City Farm has goats, guinea pigs, and lambs. In summer the Lakeside Café serves ice cream and drinks. *Phoenix Park, Dublin West, tel. 01/677–1425, www.dublinzoo.ie. €9.80. Mar.–Oct., Mon.–Sat. 9:30–6, Sun. 10:30–6; Nov.–Feb., Mon.–Sat. 9:30–5, Sun. 10:30–5.*

Both the president of Ireland and the U.S. ambassador have official residences in the park (the president's is known as Aras an Uachtarain), but neither building is open to the public. Also within the park is a **visitor center,** in the 17th-century fortified Ashtown Castle; it has information about the park's history, flora, and fauna. *Phoenix Park, Dublin West, tel. 01/677–0095, www.heritageireland.ie. €2.55. Apr.–May, daily 9:30–5:30; June–Sept., daily 10–6; Oct., daily 10–5; Nov.–mid-Mar., weekends 9:30–4:30; mid–end Mar., daily 9:30–5.*

NEED A BREAK? Just before the entrance to Phoenix Park, **RYAN'S PUB** (28 Parkgate St., Dublin West, tel. 01/677–6097) is one of Dublin's last remaining genuine, late-Victorian-era pubs.

## In This Chapter

Prices 81 • CITY CENTER (Southside) 82 • TEMPLE BAR 91 •
SOUTH CITY CENTER: BALLSBRIDGE, DONNYBROOK, AND
STILLORGAN 94 • CITY CENTER (Northside) 95 • PUB FOOD 97

*Updated by Graham Bolger*

# eating out

**DINING OUT HAS BECOME** something of a national pastime in Ireland. With the blossoming economy of the past seven or eight years, now 30 percent of all food eaten is consumed outside the home—a trend that's not confined to Dublin. The dining *experience*, too, has exploded to new levels. Ireland has always been ranked high for its pub culture—world-renowned Guinness and Irish whiskies, and good, wholesome pub grub—but now it's fast becoming a serious contender on the international restaurant scene.

The renaissance in Irish dining is due in no small way to the wave of talented young chefs who are cooking with new levels of imagination and innovation. Chefs have become celebrities on the Irish circuit, many having trained in the best kitchens at home and the world over. They have put a new blas (Irish for gloss) on traditional ingredients. You'll still find the humble Irish spud (potato) featured in all sorts of ways, accompanying wild salmon and other seafood, tender lamb, beef, and pork. You'll also find them in potato cakes and boxty, as well as in colcannon, a traditional Irish dish—with bacon and corned beef—that's a must.

Being an agricultural country, Ireland benefits from a copious supply of freshly grown produce, as well as a pure water supply. Meats are plentiful: you'll find lots of excellent Irish beef, pork, ham, and lamb. Keep an eye out, too, for seasonal specials, such as wild and farmed quail and pheasant. And, of course, there are rich and delicious seafood harvests. Consequently, you can expect to find fresh and smoked salmon, oysters, mussels, and shellfish in many guises vying with tender cuts of meat and an appetizing selection of quality vegetables on most menus. Excellent dairy products are also essential to Irish cuisine—dollops of fresh cream with home-baked desserts promise some exciting conclusions to these feasts. Have no doubt, however, that the native cheeses are the finale. Don't miss out on these. You'll find mature cheddars and blue cheeses, the slightly sweet Dubliner, St. Tola goat's cheese from Clare, and Carrigburne Brie from Wexford—only a few of the many fine artisan cheeses produced around the country.

Being an isolated island nation, the Irish love to travel abroad—foreign holidays are now the norm for most of the population. The wonderful thing is that such travel has broadened the tastes and culinary preferences of the nation, and these changes are reflected in the choice of eateries that now abound both in the capital and in other cities.

If you want ethnic food, you'll have no problem finding an establishment to suit your pocket and palette. There are elegant restaurants, stylish bistros, relaxed hideaways, and late-night eateries from which to choose. Indulge in superb French or Italian food one day, and fusion the next—you'll find that menus are influenced by Asian, Mediterranean, and other cultures. Vegetarian dishes are becoming more varied with each passing year.

The Irish dine later than Americans. They stay up later, too, so bookings are usually not taken before 6:30 or 7 PM and are made until around 11 PM. Lunch goes from 12:30 to 2:30. Pubs often serve food all day—until 8:30 or 9 PM. The Irish are an informal bunch, so smart casual dress is typical. The more select restaurants, however, do expect you to wear a jacket and tie. Shorts and sneakers are out. Check when booking if unsure.

Included here are some of the city's best addresses for a hearty pub lunch, which is where you'll now find a lot of Dubliners dining. Soups and sandwiches, hot pots, salmon, salads, and carvery joints are the usual bill of fare—along with the ubiquitous roast, mash, or chips. And while you're in Dublin, do indulge, at least once, in the traditional Irish breakfast (often served until lunchtime). It includes rashers (bacon), sausages, black and white pudding (a type of sausage), mushrooms, tomato, and a fried egg—with lots of traditional homemade brown and soda breads and the famous Irish creamery butter.

## Prices

Value Added Tax (VAT)—a 12.5% tax on food and a government excise tax on drinks  will automatically be added to your bill. Before paying, check to see whether service has been included. If it has been included, you can pay it with a credit card; but if it has not, it's more considerate to the staff to leave the tip in cash (10% to 15%) if paying the main bill by credit card.

A word of warning—you will pay for your dining pleasure here: high overheads and staffing costs have pushed up prices, especially in upscale places. The good news is that, although Dublin doesn't have Starbucks, there are scores of local cafés serving excellent coffee, often with a good sandwich. Small bakeries are beginning to spring up, borrowing trends from all around the world, offering inexpensive pizzas, focaccia, pitas, tacos, and wraps (taking over from the sandwich as the favorite snack).

It's worthwhile to see if the restaurant of your choice offers an early bird and/or pre- or post-theater menu, with significantly lower set prices at specific times, often from 6 to 7:30 PM.

| CATEGORY | THE REPUBLIC* |
| --- | --- |
| $$$$ | over €29 |
| $$$ | €22–€29 |
| $$ | €13–€21 |
| $ | under €13 |

*per person for a main course at dinner

## CITY CENTER (SOUTHSIDE)
### AMERICAN
**\$\$\$–\$\$\$\$ SHANAHANS.** Dublin's first American-style steak house, in an elegant Georgian building, proves to be a huge success. It's an old-style place—think large fireplaces, gilt mirrors, a deep carpet, and elegant chandeliers. Certified Irish Angus beef is the star dish, though seafood and lamb are also prized. The basement bar—the Oval Office—is full of Americana and presidential paperwork. 119 St. Stephen's Green, City Center, tel. 01/407–0939. Reservations essential. AE, DC, MC, V. No lunch.

### CONTEMPORARY
**\$\$\$\$ PEACOCK ALLEY.** This elegant, modern restaurant with a large,
★ airy 120-seat room commands a spectacular view over St. Stephen's Green at one end and the white-tiled open kitchen at the other. Strikingly inventive dishes include smoked salmon with basmati rice, pear, preserved ginger, soy sauce, and quesadilla; deep-fried crab cakes with *katafi* (shredded phyllo pastry); and daube of pot-roasted beef. Service is excellent, and there's a strong wine list—well suited to the type of food served here. Fitzwilliam Hotel, St. Stephen's Green, City Center, tel. 01/478–7015. Reservations essential. AE, DC, MC, V. Closed Tues.

**\$\$\$ COOKE'S CAFÉ.** Johnny Cooke's Mediterranean bistro is a cool spot for visiting movie stars. Sit out in summer under an awning and people-watch while you enjoy elegantly presented dishes— on huge, white Wedgwood plates. Favorites include pasta with a rich, bubbling Gorgonzola sauce; lobster simply grilled with garlic-herb butter; salad with pieces of tender roast duck; and crab salad with spinach, coriander, mango salsa, and lime dressing. Don't come if you're in a hurry, because the service, through charming, is slow. 14 S. William St., City Center, tel. 01/679–0536. Reservations essential. AE, DC, MC, V. Closed Sun.–Mon.

**\$–\$\$\$ LA STAMPA.** It's one of the most dramatic dining rooms in Dublin,
★ with huge gilt mirrors and elaborate candelabra that are gloriously over the top. This gives even the simplest meal a sense of fun and

occasion. The menu changes frequently, and reflects the restaurant's eclectic, international style. Get rack of organic lamb with braised beans, tomatoes, and rosemary jus; roast scallops with artichoke mash and a tomato vinaigrette; or giant prawns served with garlic or mango mayonnaise. Expect brisk but friendly service. *35 Dawson St., City Center, tel. 01/677–8611. AE, DC, MC, V.*

## CONTINENTAL

**$$$–$$$$** **LOCKS.** A genuinely warm welcome awaits you at Claire Douglas's town-house restaurant, which overlooks the Grand Canal. The dining room is comfortable and old-fashioned, with banquette seating and starched table linens. Hearty portions are served on antique ironstone plates. Classic starters include Locks's special potato skins—dished up with prawns, tomato, and spinach with a fabulous hollandaise sauce—and excellent smoked salmon. Choose your main course from the traditional fish dishes, Irish lamb, and venison. *1 Windsor Terr., Portobello, South of the Liffey, tel. 01/454–3391. Reservations essential. AE, DC, MC, V. Closed Sun.*

**$$–$$$** **BROWNES BRASSERIE.** Go to this Georgian town house, now a boutique hotel on St. Stephen's Green, if you're looking for a lovely spot in which to share an intimate meal. Huge mirrors reflect the light from crystal chandeliers onto the jewel-colored walls and upholstery. The rich and heartwarming food includes such classics as pan-seared scallops and black pudding on beet-root marmalade. Treat yourself to the lavender-scented crème brûlée. *22 St. Stephen's Green, City Center, tel. 01/638–3939. Reservations essential. AE, DC, MC, V. No lunch Sat.*

## ETHNIC

**$$** **KHYBER TANDOORI.** Take a short walk from St. Stephen's Green to this gem of a restaurant. It specializes in Pakistani cuisine, but also serves a broad range of Indian dishes. Try the shami (Syrian) kebabs—dainty, spiced patties of minced lamb and lentils—or *kabuli chicken tikka shashlik*, marinated, diced chicken with onions and red and green peppers, which comes bright red and sizzling on an iron platter. Settle in and admire the richly embroidered

# dublin dining

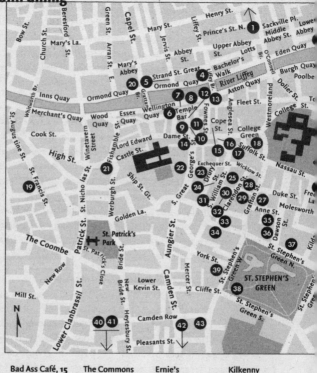

Bad Ass Café, 15

Beaufield
Mews, 49

Belgo, 7

Brownes
Brasserie, 37

Bruno's, 6

Burdock's, 21

Chapter One, 1

The Commons
Restaurant, 38

Cooke's Café, 24

Diep le
Shaker, 46

Dish, 10

Dobbins, 47

Eden, 12

Elephant &
Castle, 13

Ernie's
Restaurant, 50

Halo, 5

Harbour
Master, 3

Il Primo, 43

Jaipur, 31

Khyber
Tandoori, 32

Kilkenny
Kitchen, 44

La Stampa, 36

Lemon Crêpe and
Coffee Co., 25

Les Frères
Jacques, 9

Locks, 41

Mao, 28

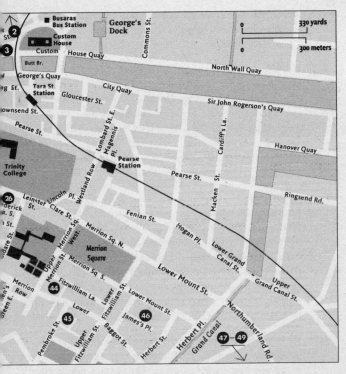

| Mermaid Café, 14 | Osteria Romano, 11 | The Steps of Rome, 33 | **Pub Food** |
| Milano, 35 | Pasta Fresca, 29 | The Tea Room, 4 | Davy Byrne's, 27 |
| Nude, 17 | Patrick Guilbaud, 45 | Thornton's, 40 | Old Stand, 23 |
| O'Connells, 48 | Peacock Alley, 30 | Wagamama, 34 | O'Neill's, 18 |
| Old Dublin, 19 | Shanahans, 39 | Yamamori, 22 | Stag's Head, 16 |
| One Pico, 42 | Soup Dragon, 20 | | Zanzibar, 4 |
| 101 Talbot, 2 | | | |

wall hangings and the great gusts of steam coming from the tandoori oven in the glassed-in area. 44–45 S. William St., City Center, tel. 01/670–4855. AE, DC, MC, V. No lunch Sun.

**$–$$ JAIPUR.** A spacious room with a sweeping staircase and contemporary furnishings reflect the modern, cutting-edge approach to Indian cooking. Mixed with more traditional dishes, such as chicken tikka masala, you'll find the more unusual *matka gosdh* (lamb dish) on offer. Dishes can be toned down (or spiced up) to suit your palate, and service is courteous and prompt. The wine list is well thought out. 41 S Great George's St., City Center, tel. 01/677–0999. Reservations essential. AE, MC, V.

### FRENCH

**$$$$ PATRICK GUILBAUD.** Expect superb cooking and impeccable
★ service at this fine restaurant with a marvelously lofty dining room hung with paintings from the owners' private collection. The best dishes here are simple—and flawless. Try the house specialty, Chalons duck à l'orange. Follow that, if you can, with the *assiette au chocolat* (a plate of five hot and cold chocolate desserts). The wine list spans 70 pages. 21 Upper Merrion St., South of the Liffey, tel. 01/676–4192. Reservations essential. AE, DC, MC, V. Closed Sun.–Mon.

**$$$$ THORNTON'S.** If you are passionate about food, this place is
★ mandatory—owner Kevin Thornton has forged a reputation as one of the very best chefs in Ireland. The upstairs dining room is simply decorated—there's little to distract you from the exquisite food. Thornton's cooking style is light, and his dishes are small masterpieces of structural engineering. In season, he marinates legs of partridge, then debones and reforms the bird, with the breasts shaped into a crown. Desserts range from banana ice cream to fig tartlet. Sheridans of Dublin supplies the enormous selection of cheeses. 1 Portobello Rd., South of the Liffey, tel. 01/454–9067. Reservations essential. AE, DC, MC, V. Closed Sun.–Mon. No lunch Tues.–Thurs.

**$ LEMON CRÊPE AND COFFEE CO.** They've got the best crêpes in town, and hungry Dubliners know it. The space is compact, white, and minimalist. A few pavement tables—complete with an outdoor heater—make this a great spot for a tasty snack while you watch Dublin saunter by. To really indulge, follow up savory pancakes with sugar-sweet crêpes. Takeout service is swift. 66 S. William St., City Center, tel. 01/672–9044. No credit cards.

### IRISH

**$$$$ THE COMMONS RESTAURANT.** This large, elegant dining room is in the basement of Newman House. The patio doors open onto a paved courtyard—ideal for for summer aperitifs and alfresco lunches. Typical dishes include ravioli of artichoke with truffles and asparagus. If you have time, take a stroll in the nearby Iveagh Gardens, an enclosed park that's one of Dublin's best-kept secrets. 85–86 St. Stephen's Green, City Center, tel. 01/478–0530. Reservations essential. AE, DC, MC, V. No lunch Sat. Closed Sun.

**$$–$$$ DOBBINS.** Don't be deceived by the sawdust on the floor and the simple furnishings. The combination of cozy booth seating, friendly service, and classic bistro food make Dobbins popular with businesspeople. Owner John O'Byrne presides over an impressive cellar with hundreds of wines from around the world. Tempura of prawns is a popular starter; boned brace of quail with black pudding (sausage with dried pig's blood) and foie gras stuffing is a typical entrée. There's valet parking, and the staff is expert at summoning taxis. 15 Stephens La., off Mount St., City Center, tel. 01/676–4679. Reservations essential. AE, DC, MC, V. Closed Mon.

**$$–$$$ ONE PICO.** Not only is the design sophisticated and modern, but Eamonn O'Reilly's cooking is decidedly contemporary. Dishes such as fresh chicken and kale-and-bacon mashed potato demonstrate a savvy use of Irish ingredients. Follow this with the baked chèvre cheesecake with praline chocolate and orange confit. Service is excellent, and the top-class cooking makes this good value for the money. 5–6 Moleswotrh Pl., Schoolhouse Lane, South of the Liffey, tel. 01/676–0300. Reservations essential. AE, DC, MC, V. No lunch weekends.

**$ BURDOCK'S.** Join the inevitable queue at Dublin's famous take-out fish-and-chips shop, right next door to the Lord Edward. Eat in the gardens of St. Patrick's Cathedral, a five-minute walk away. 21 Werburgh St., City Center, tel. 01/454–0306. No credit cards.

**$ KILKENNY KITCHEN.** Take a break from shopping and sightseeing at this big self-service restaurant on the upper floor of the Kilkenny Shop. Homemade soup, casseroles, cold meats, and salads are arranged on a long buffet, along with lots of tasty breads and cakes. Try to get a table by the window overlooking the playing fields of Trinity College. Lunchtime is busy, but it's very pleasant for morning coffee or afternoon tea. 5–6 Nassau St., City Center, tel. 01/677–7066. AE, DC, MC, V.

**$ SOUP DRAGON.** This tiny café and take-out soup shop serves an astonishing array of fresh soups daily. Soups come in three sizes, and you can get vegetarian soup or soups with meat- or fish-based broth. Favorites include red pepper, tomato, and goat cheese soup; fragrant Thai chicken soup; and hearty mussel, potato, and leek soup. The friendly staff make fine coffee and delicious smoothies. The cost of soup includes bread and a piece of fruit for dessert—an excellent value. 168 Capel St., North of the Liffey, tel. 01/872–3277. No credit cards. No dinner. Closed Sun.

### ITALIAN
**$–$$$ IL PRIMO.** Old wooden tables and chairs give this place a casual feel, and the friendly, if cramped, surroundings attracts a devoted clientele. The Irish-Italian cuisine is both imaginative and reassuring. Among the main courses, a delicious chicken ravioli in white wine cream, with Parma ham and wild mushrooms, is a standout. There's a very long wine list specializing in Italian wines. Montague St., off Harcourt St., South of the Liffey, tel. 01/478–3373. AE, DC, MC, V. No lunch weekends.

**$–$$$ PASTA FRESCA.** This stylish little Italian restaurant and deli off Grafton Street squeezes a surprising number of people into a fairly small space. Antipasto *misto* (assorted sliced Italian meats) makes a good appetizer—or go for carpaccio *della casa* (wafer-thin slices of beef fillet, with fresh Parmesan, olive oil, lemon juice, and black pepper). The main courses consist of Pasta Fresca's own very good versions of well-known dishes, such as spaghetti *alla Bolognese*, cannelloni, and lasagna *al forno*. The pasta is freshly made each day. Lines form at lunchtime. *3–4 Chatham St., City Center, tel. 01/679–2402. AE, DC, MC, V.*

**$ MILANO.** The big open kitchen at this bright, cheerful place turns out a wide array of tasty, flashy pizzas with combinations like tomato and mozzarella, ham and egg, Cajun with prawns and Tabasco, spinach and egg, or ham and anchovy. There are also simple salads, such as tomato and mozzarella with dough balls, and some baked pasta dishes. This is a good place to dine late, with last orders at midnight. Two other branches have opened up, one in Temple Bar and another on Bachelors Walk along the Quays. *38 Dawson St., City Center, tel. 01/670–7744; 18 Essex St. E, Temple Bar, tel. 01/670–3384; 38–39 Lower Ormond Quay, North of the Liffey, tel. 01/872–0003. AE, DC, MC, V.*

**$ THE STEPS OF ROME.** Just a few steps from Grafton Street, it's perfect for a late-night bite or quick lunch (or takeout). Slices of delicious, thin base, homemade pizza, with all the traditional toppings, are the main attraction. The mushroom pizza (*fungi*) is particularly good. The handful of tables is usually full, but it's worth waiting for the classic Italian pasta dishes—pasta parmigiano or pesto, and good, fresh salads with focaccia. Follow it up with ice cream or tiramisu, and good, strong espresso. *1 Chatham Ct., City Center, tel. 01/670–5630. No credit cards.*

### JAPANESE

**$–$$ YAMAMORI.** The first of many Ramen noodle bars to open in Ireland, this is one of the best. The meals-in-a-bowl are a splendid slurping experience, and although you will be supplied with a small

Chinese-style soup spoon, the best approach is with chopsticks. You can also get sushi and sashimi, and delicious chicken teriyaki. *71–72 S. Great George's St., City Center, tel. 01/475–5001. AE, MC, V.*

**$ WAGAMAMA.** Modeled on a Japanese canteen, the long wooden tables and benches ensure a unique communal dining experience. This low-ceilinged basement noodle bar is constantly packed, but service is swift. Formal courses aren't acknowledged—food is served as soon as it's ready, and appetizers and main courses arrive together. Choose from filling bowls of Cha Han (fried rice with chicken, prawns, and vegtables) or chili beef Ramen, and wash it down with fresh fruit or vegetable juices. *S. King St., City Center, tel. 01/478–2152. AE, DC, MC, V.*

### PAN-ASIAN

**$–$$$ DIEP LE SHAKER.** Slightly off the beaten track, on a narrow lane off Pembroke Street, this big, flamboyant Thai food spot was an instant success when it opened. Comfortable high-back chairs, pristine table linen, and elegant stemware make it a lovely, and posh, place to dine. Know in advance that it's a place where half the reason for going is to see and be seen. Try the steamed scallops and ginger, or lobster in garlic pepper and Thai herbs. Don't be surprised to see people ordering champagne to go with their meal—there's a permanent party feel here, which attracts Ireland's wealthy in droves. *55 Pembroke La., City Center, tel. 01/661–1829. AE, DC, MC, V. Closed Sun.*

**$–$$ MAO.** Everything is Asian fusion at this bustling café, from the little Andy Warhol pastiche of Chairman Mao on the washroom door to the eclectic mix of dishes on the menu, which combine influences of Thai, Vietnamese, and other Southeast Asian cuisines. Favorites are the Malaysian chicken and the Nasi Goreng (Indonesian fried rice with chicken and shrimp). Reservations aren't accepted, so go early to be sure of a seat. There's another branch in Dun Laoghaire, a 20-minute taxi ride from the city center. *2 Chatham Row, City Center, tel. 01/670–4899; The Pavilion, Dun Laoghaire, South County Dublin, tel. 01/214–8090. MC, V.*

### RUSSIAN

**$$–$$$ OLD DUBLIN.** This brasserie-style restaurant near St. Patrick's Cathedral specializes in Russian and Scandinavian food. In the evening, glowing fires warm the cozy-but-elegant low-ceilinged rooms; tables are candlelit. You'll find familiar dishes: blini, borscht, chicken Kiev, and beef Stroganoff, but also a few Irish staples, such as roast lamb and fresh baked salmon. One fine surprise on the menu is planked sirloin Hussar, a steak baked between two oak planks, served on an oak platter with salad and sweet pickle. *90–91 St. Francis St., City Center, tel. 01/454–2028. AE, DC, MC, V. Closed Sun. No lunch Mon., Tues., Sat.*

### VEGETARIAN

**$ NUDE.** This sleek fast-food café was such a good idea that owner Norman Hewson—brother of U2's Bono—has opened another branch for takeout only. The menu is mostly vegetarian, and everything on it is made with organic and free-range ingredients. Choose from homemade soups and vegetable wraps, smoothies, and fresh-squeezed juices. *21 Suffolk St., City Center, tel. 01/677–4804. AE, DC, MC, V.*

## TEMPLE BAR
### AMERICAN/CASUAL

**$–$$$ BELGO.** It's part of a Belgian chain of restaurants, and perfect if you want a large serving of comfort food and are prepared to be adventurous with what you drink. They have dozens of beers, and the french fries, served alongside omelets, burgers, *saucissons* (large, flavored Belgian sausages), and steaks, are the best you'll eat in Temple Bar. *17–19 Sycamore St., Temple Bar, tel. 01/672–7554. AE, DC, MC, V.*

**$–$$$ ELEPHANT & CASTLE.** One of Temple Bar's most popular and established eateries, Elephant & Castle serves traditional American food—charcoal-grilled burgers, salads, omelets, sandwiches, and pasta. Sunday brunch is always packed. When the service is good, the turnover tends to be quick, although you may be inclined to linger. Generous portions of unfussy and well-prepared food, and the casual environment, make this a Dublin standout. New Yorkers take note: yes, this is a cousin of the restaurant of the same name in Greenwich Village. *18 Temple Bar, tel. 01/679–3121. Reservations not accepted. AE, DC, MC, V.*

**$–$$  BAD ASS CAFÉ.** Sinéad O'Connor used to wait tables at this lively café in a converted warehouse between the Central Bank and Ha'penny Bridge. (A "Rock 'n Stroll" tour plaque notes O'Connor's past here.) Old-fashioned cash shuttles whiz around the ceiling of the barnlike space, with bare floors and painted in primary colors inside and out. You can indulge in some great people-watching behind the wall of glass here. The food—mainly pizzas and burgers—is unexceptional, but the Bad Ass can be a lot of fun and appetites of all ages love it. *9–11 Crown Alley, Temple Bar, tel. 01/671–2596. AE, MC, V.*

### CONTEMPORARY

**$$$$  THE TEA ROOM.** If you have something to celebrate or you're hoping to spot some celebrities, this is a good bet. It's part of the Clarence hotel, where the stars of stage and screen stay when they're in town. The bright, lofty dining room has spectacular flower arrangements and elegant, modern table settings. The food is adventurous and consistently good. Typically mouthwatering entrées include risotto of mussels and courgettes with parsley and garlic. *Clarence hotel, 6–8 Wellington Quay, Temple Bar, tel. 01/407–0813. Reservations essential. AE, DC, MC, V.*

**$$–$$$  EDEN.** The young owners of several of Dublin's café-style bars,
★  including the Front Lounge and the Globe, have followed those successes with a popular brasserie-style restaurant with an open kitchen and high wall of glass looking out onto one of Temple Bar's main squares. Patio-style doors lead to an outdoor eating area—a major plus in a city with relatively few alfresco dining spots. Have no doubt: Eden is a happening, trendy place, hip with fashion and media types. Standout dishes include duck leg confit with lentils, and mustard-crusted braised hock of ham served with *champ*

(creamy, buttery mashed potatoes with scallions). Desserts include rhubarb crème brûlée and homemade ice creams and sorbets. *Meeting House Sq., Temple Bar, tel. 01/670–5372. Reservations essential.* AE, DC, MC, V.

**$$–$$$** **MERMAID CAFÉ.** One of the chef-owners dabbles in fine art, and his tastes in this area are reflected in his artistic and decorative style of bistro cooking. It's not cheap, but the food is quite good. Lunch is an exceptional value—piquant crab cakes, hearty seafood casseroles, venison sausage, or radicchio and melted goat's cheese. Good attention to detail and a thoughtful wine list make this modest restaurant with tall windows looking onto busy Dame Street one of the most popular eateries in Temple Bar. *69 Dame St., Temple Bar, tel. 01/670–8236. MC, V.*

**$–$$** **DISH.** Clever cuisine, a relaxed dining room, and pleasant staff have secured Dish a loyal following. The large white room with sanded floorboards, oversized mirrors, and industrial piping is a wonderfully stylish space in which to enjoy Gerard Foote's confident cooking. Dishes range from grilled Clonakilty black pudding with roast red pepper and borlotti beans to roast monkfish with bacon, savoy cabbage, beetroot, and cream. The focus is on Irish ingredients. It's popular for Sunday brunch, and the midweek lunch is also an excellent value. *2 Crow St., Temple Bar, tel. 01/671–1248. Reservations essential. AE, DC, MC, V.*

### FRENCH

**$$$–$$$$** **LES FRÈRES JACQUES.** It brings a little bit of Paris to Temple Bar:
★ old prints of Paris and Deauville hang on the green-papered walls, and the French waiters, dressed in white Irish linen and black bow ties, exude a Gallic charm without being excessively formal. Expect traditional French cooking that nods to the seasons. Seafood is a major attraction, and lobster, fished right from the tank, is a specialty—it's typically roasted and flambéed with Irish whiskey. Also recommended are the meat and game specialties, when in season. A piano player performs Friday and Saturday evenings and the occasional weeknight. *74 Dame St., Temple Bar,*

tel. 01/679–4555. *Reservations essential. AE, MC, V. Closed Sun. No lunch Sat.*

## ITALIAN

**$$–$$$ OSTERIA ROMANO.** Members of the Italian community congregate in the evenings at this cheerful eatery, which serves authentic Roman cuisine. Specialties include *melanzane parmigiani*, a delicious dish of baked eggplant and cheese, and the excellent cream-based pastas, such as spaghetti Alfredo and carbonara. Beware of finishing the meal with too many flaming *sambucas* (anise-flavored, semisweet Italian liqueur). The best table, by the window, overlooks the street. *5 Crow St., Temple Bar, tel. 01/670–8662. AE, DC, MC, V.*

## MEDITERRANEAN

**$$–$$$ BRUNO'S.** Experienced French-born restaurateur Bruno Berta has a hit on his hands with his French-Mediterranean bistro on one of the busiest corners in Temple Bar. Simple but stylish dishes range from starters like feuilleté of crab meat and saffron sauce to main dishes of roast scallops with Jerusalem artichoke purée and warm smoked bacon and walnut dressing. The friendly service and relaxed surroundings make this one of the area's best bets. *30 Essex St. E, Temple Bar, tel. 01/670–6767. AE, DC, MC, V. Closed Sun.*

# SOUTH CITY CENTER: BALLSBRIDGE, DONNYBROOK, AND STILLORGAN

## CONTEMPORARY

**$$ O'CONNELLS.** Fresh Irish produce and baked goods are the emphasis in this vast, modern space with sleek timber paneling and floor-to-ceiling windows. Go for the spit-roasted chicken or anything baked in the huge clay oven. Other tasty dishes include a warm salad of kidneys with greens and oyster mushrooms, and monkfish with a lively pepper, tomato, and coriander salsa. A tremendous array of fresh breads is on display in the open kitchen, which turns into a buffet for breakfast and lunch. *Merrion Rd., Ballsbridge, South County Dublin, tel. 01/647–3304. AE, DC, MC, V.*

## CONTINENTAL

**$$–$$$  BEAUFIELD MEWS.** The original cobbled courtyard and the 18th-century coach house, with stables, wonderfully, remain. The place is even said to be haunted by a friendly monk. Inside it's all black beams, old furniture, and bric-a-brac. The more desirable tables overlook the courtyard or the garden or are, less predictably, "under the nun" (the nun in question is a 17th-century portrait). While the main attraction is the surroundings, the food, based on fresh ingredients, will keep you coming back—old favorites include roast duckling à l'orange and grilled wild-salmon steaks. The restaurant is a 10-mi taxi ride from the city center. *Woodlands Ave., Stillorgan, South County Dublin, tel. 01/288–0375. Reservations essential. AE, DC, MC, V. No dinner Sun., closed Mon.*

## IRISH

**$$$–$$$$  ERNIE'S RESTAURANT.** High-quality ingredients, attention to detail, and consistency are the hallmarks of this long-established and welcoming restaurant, built around a large tree and fountain. Blue Irish linen and sparkling crystal decorate the tables. The seasonal menu always has a variety of catches of the day—grilled sole with spring onion and thyme butter, or poached wild salmon on a bed of creamed potato. You can also expect four or five meat and poultry entrées, such as roasted rack of Wicklow lamb with a caramelized onion tart. Ernie's is only a few minutes by taxi from the city center. *Mulberry Gardens, Donnybrook, South County Dublin, tel. 01/269–3300. AE, DC, MC, V. Closed Sun.–Mon. and 1 wk at Christmas. No lunch weekends.*

# CITY CENTER (NORTHSIDE)
## CONTEMPORARY

**$$$  CHAPTER ONE.** In the vaulted, stone-walled basement of the Dublin Writers Museum, just down the street from the Hugh Lane Municipal Gallery of Modern Art, is one of the most notable restaurants in northside Dublin. Try the roast venison with mustard and herb lentils, pancetta, and chestnut dumpling, and roast beetroot. The rich bread-and-butter pudding is a stellar dessert.

*18–19 Parnell Sq., North of the Liffey, tel. 01/873–2266. Reservations essential. AE, DC, MC, V. Closed Sun.–Mon. No lunch Sat.*

**\$\$–\$\$\$**    **HALO.** This restaurant in the chic Morrison hotel has been an instant hit with the fashion crowd and lawyers from the nearby Four Courts. The dramatic dining room with a soaring ceiling and minimalist decor, devised by fashion designer John Rocha, looks moody and mysterious by night, and a little forbidding by day. The emphasis is on complex dishes that look as good as they taste: seared, cured salmon on creamed spinach, and *pomme vapour* (mashed potatoes) with coriander are among the specialties. Desserts are miniature works of art on enormous China platters. *Morrison hotel, Ormond Quay, North of the Liffey, tel. 01/887–2421. AE, DC, MC, V.*

**\$–\$\$**    **HARBOUR MASTER.** The main attraction of this big, airy restaurant and bar in the Irish Financial Services Centre north of the Liffey is its setting: it overlooks a canal basin. At lunch the place is packed with stockbrokers and lawyers; dinner is more subdued. You can dine bistro-style at the cavernous bar, but it's better to head for the more spacious—and relaxing—newly built section, which serves hearty prawn linguine with cashews, and beef and Guinness stew. *Custom House Docks, North of the Liffey, tel. 01/670–1688. AE, DC, MC, V.*

## MEDITERRANEAN

**\$–\$\$**    **101 TALBOT.** Popular with Dublin's artistic and literary set, and conveniently close to the Abbey and Gate theaters, this comfortable upstairs restaurant showcases an ever-changing exhibition of local artists' work. The creative, contemporary food—with Mediterranean and Middle Eastern influences—uses fresh, local ingredients. Try the roast pork fillet marinated in orange, ginger, and soy, and served with fried noodles. The cashew and red-pepper rissoles with chili and ginger jam, served with wild and basmati rice, also impresses. Healthy options and several vegetarian choices make this a highly versatile restaurant. *101 Talbot*

St., North of the Liffey, tel. 01/874–5011. Reservations essential. AE, DC, MC, V. Closed Sun.–Mon.

## PUB FOOD

Most pubs serve food at lunchtime, some throughout the day. Food ranges from hearty soups and stews to chicken curries, smoked-salmon salads, and sandwiches, and much of it is surprisingly good. Expect to pay €6–€10 for a main course. Some of the larger, more popular pubs may take credit cards.

**DAVY BYRNE'S.** James Joyce immortalized this pub in *Ulysses*. Nowadays it's more akin to a cocktail bar than a Dublin pub, but it's good for fresh and smoked salmon, salads, and a hot daily special. *21 Duke St., City Center, tel. 01/671–1298.*

**OLD STAND.** It's conveniently close to Grafton Street, and serves grilled food, including steaks. *37 Exchequer St., City Center, tel. 01/677–7220.*

**O'NEILL'S.** This fine pub, a stone's throw from Trinity College, has the best carvery of any pub in the city. (Immensely popular in Ireland, a carvery is meat cut to order—you pick the joint, they carve for you as much of it as you can eat. It comes with vegetables or potatoes and gravy.) A hearty lunch, served between noon and 2:30, costs about €6.35–€7.60. *2 Suffolk St., City Center, tel. 01/670–5755.*

**STAG'S HEAD.** Serving one of Dublin's best pub lunches, this place is a favorite among both Trinity students and businesspeople. *1 Dame Ct., City Center, tel. 01/679–3701.*

**ZANZIBAR.** This spectacular, immense bar on the north side of the Liffey looks as though it might be more at home in downtown Marrakesh. Laze away an afternoon in one of the wicker chairs and enjoy hearty, freshly made sandwiches, salads, and cocktails. *34–35 Lower Ormond Quay, North of the Liffey, tel. 01/878–7212.*

## IN THIS CHAPTER

SHOPPING STREETS 99 • SHOPPING CENTERS 102 •
DEPARTMENT STORES 104 • OUTDOOR MARKETS 105 •
SPECIALTY SHOPS 106 • Antiques 106 • Books 106 • China,
Crystal, Ceramics, and Jewelry 108 • Museum Stores 109 •
Music 110 • Sweaters and Tweeds 110 • Vintage 111

*Updated by Anto Howard*

# shopping

**THE ONLY KNOWN SPECIMENS** of leprechauns or shillelaghs in Ireland are those in souvenir-shop windows, and shamrocks mainly bloom around the borders of Irish linen handkerchiefs and tablecloths. But today you'll find way more than kitschy designs. There's a tremendous variety of stores in Dublin, many of which are quite sophisticated—as a walk through Dublin's central shopping area, from O'Connell to Grafton Street, will prove. Department stores stock internationally known fashion-designer goods and housewares, and small (and often pricey) boutiques sell Irish crafts and other merchandise. But don't expect too many bargains here. And be prepared, if you're shopping in central Dublin, to push through crowds—especially in the afternoons and on weekends. Most large shops and department stores are open Monday–Saturday 9–6. Although nearly all department stores are closed on Sunday, some smaller specialty shops stay open. Those with later closing hours are noted below. You're particularly likely to find sales in January, February, July, and August.

## SHOPPING STREETS

Dublin's dozen or so main shopping streets each have a different character. Visit them all to appreciate the wide range of items for sale here. The main commercial streets north of the river have both chain and department stores that tend to be less expensive (and less design-conscious) than their counterparts in the city center on the other side of the Liffey.

## City Center (Northside)

**HENRY STREET.** Cash-conscious Dubliners shop on Henry Street, which runs westward from O'Connell Street. Arnotts department store is the anchor; smaller, specialty stores sell CDs, footwear, and clothing. Henry Street's continuation, Mary Street, has a branch of Marks & Spencer and the Jervis Shopping Centre.

**O'CONNELL STREET.** One of Dublin's largest department stores, Cleiy's, faces the GPO across the city's main thoroughfare— more downscale than southside city streets (such as Grafton St.) but still worth a walk. On the same side of the street as the post office is Eason's, a large book, magazine, and stationery store.

## City Center (Southside)

**DAWSON STREET.** Just east of Grafton Street between Nassau Street to the north and St. Stephen's Green to the south, you'll find the city's primary bookstore avenue. Waterstone's and Hodges Figgis face each other on different sides of the street.

**FRANCIS STREET.** The Liberties, the oldest part of the city, is the hub of Dublin's antiques trade. This street and surrounding areas, such as the Coombe, have plenty of shops where you can browse. If you're looking for something in particular, dealers will gladly recommend the appropriate store to you.

**GRAFTON STREET.** Dublin's bustling pedestrian-only main shopping street has two upscale department stores: Marks & Spencer and Brown Thomas. The rest of the street is taken up by smaller shops, many of them branches of international chains, such as the Body Shop and Bally, and many British chains. This is also the spot to buy fresh flowers, available at reasonable prices from a number of outdoor stands. On the smaller streets off Grafton Street, especially Duke Street, South Anne Street, and Chatham Street, you'll find worthwhile crafts, clothing, and designer housewares shops.

# dublin shopping

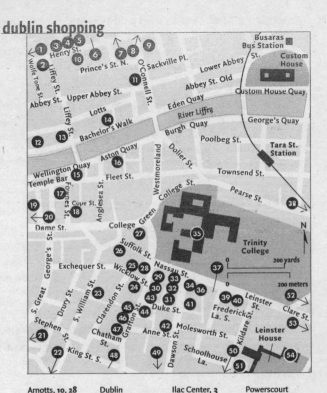

Arnotts, **10, 28**
An Táin, **15**
A-Wear, **7, 44**
Blarney Woollen
Mills, **37**
Books Upstairs, **27**
Brown Thomas, **24**
Cathach Books, **31**
Celtic Note, **39**
Claddagh
Records, **17**
Cleo Ltd., **49**
Clery's, **9**
Conlon
Antiques, **22**
Crannóg, **19**
Designyard, **20**

Dublin
Bookshop, **46**
Dublin Woollen
Mills, **13**
Dunnes
Stores, **6, 48**
Eason's, **11**
Flip, **18**
Fred Hanna's, **36**
Gael Linn, **52**
Greene's, **53**
HMV, **5, 47**
Ha'penny Bridge
Galleries, **14**
Hodges Figgis, **32**
House of
Ireland, **33**

Ilac Center, **3**
Jenny Vander, **50**
Jervis Centre, **1**
Kevin & Howlin, **34**
Kilkenny Shop, **40**
Marks &
Spencer, **2, 43**
McCullogh
Piggott, **26**
McDowell, **8**
Monaghan's, **30**
National Gallery
of Ireland
Shop, **54**
Nat'l Museum
Shop, **51**
O'Sullivan
Antiques, **21**

Powerscourt
Townhouse Ctr., **23**
Roches Stores, **1**
Royal Hibernian
Way, **42**
St. Stephen's
Green Centre, **48**
Tower Design
Ctr., **38**
Tower Records, **25**
Trinity College
Library Shop, **35**
Virgin
Megastore, **16**
Waterstone's, **41**
Weir & Sons, **29**
Westbury Mall, **45**
Winding Stair, **12**

**NASSAU STREET.** Dublin's main tourist-oriented thoroughfare has some of the best-known stores selling Irish goods, but you won't find many locals shopping here. Still, if you're looking for classic Irish gifts to take home, you should be sure at least to browse along here.

**TEMPLE BAR.** Dublin's hippest neighborhood is dotted with small, precious boutiques—mainly intimate, quirky shops that traffic in a small selection of *très* trendy goods, from vintage wear to some of the most avant-garde Irish clothing you'll find anywhere in the city.

## SHOPPING CENTERS

### City Center (Northside)

**ILAC CENTER** (Henry St., North of the Liffey) was Dublin's first large, modern shopping center, with two department stores, hundreds of specialty shops, and several restaurants. The stores are not as exclusive as at some of the other centers, but there's plenty of free parking.

The slightly high-end **JERVIS SHOPPING CENTRE** (Jervis and Mary Sts., North of the Liffey, tel. 01/878–1323) has some of the major British chain stores. It has a compact design and plenty of parking space.

### City Center (Southside)

**POWERSCOURT TOWNHOUSE CENTRE** (59 S. William St., City Center), the former town home of Lord Powerscourt, built in 1771, has an interior courtyard that has been refurbished and roofed over; a pianist often plays on the dais at ground-floor level. Coffee shops and restaurants share space with a mix of antiques and crafts stores, including the **HQ Gallery,** the main showcase of the Irish Craft Council and one of the finest places in Dublin to buy contemporary crafts. You can also buy original Irish fashions here by young designers, such as Gráinne Walsh.

**ROYAL HIBERNIAN WAY** (off Dawson St. between S. Anne and Duke Sts., City Center, tel. 01/679–5919) is on the former site of the two-centuries-old Royal Hibernian Hotel, a coaching inn that was demolished in 1983. The pricey, stylish shops—about 20 or 30, many selling fashionable clothes—are small in scale and include a branch of Leonidas, the Belgian chocolate firm.

**ST. STEPHEN'S GREEN CENTRE** (northwest corner of St. Stephen's Green, City Center, tel. 01/478–0888), Dublin's largest and most ambitious shopping center, resembles a giant greenhouse, with ironwork in the Victorian style. On three floors overlooked by a vast clock, the 100 mostly small shops sell a variety of crafts, fashions, and household goods.

**TOWER DESIGN CENTRE** (Pearse St., City Center, tel. 01/677–5655), east of the heart of the city center (near the Waterways Visitor Centre), has more than 35 separate crafts shops in a converted 1862 sugar-refinery tower. On the ground floor, you can stop at workshops devoted to heraldry and Irish pewter; the other six floors have stores that sell hand-painted silks, ceramics, hand-knit items, jewelry, and fine-art cards and prints.

**WESTBURY MALL** (Westbury Hotel, off Grafton St., City Center) is an upmarket shopping mall. Here you'll find designer jewelry, antique rugs, and decorative goods.

## County Dublin Suburbs

**BLACKROCK** (Blackrock, Co. Dublin, South County Dublin, tel. 01/283–1660), to the south, is technically outside of Dublin's city center, but it deserves special mention as one of the most customer-friendly shopping centers around. It's built on two levels, looking onto an inner courtyard, with the giant Superquinn Foodstore, cafés, and restaurants. Blackrock can be reached conveniently on the DART train line; it has its own stop.

BLANCHARDSTOWN (Blanchardstown, North County Dublin Dublin 15, tel. 01/822–1356) is the biggest shopping center in the country; you'll find plenty of families shopping here, as it's a good spot for bargains. The No. 39 bus from Lower Abbey Street goes to Blanchardstown.

## DEPARTMENT STORES

**ARNOTTS** (Henry St., North of the Liffey, tel. 01/872–1111), on three floors, stocks a wide variety of clothing, household, and sporting goods. The smaller Grafton Street branch (Grafton St., City Center, tel. 01/872–1111) sells new fashion and footwear.

**A-WEAR** (Grafton St., City Center, tel. 01/671–7200; Henry St., North of the Liffey, tel. 01/872–4644) specializes in fashion for men and women. Many of the items are seasonal and closely follow the ever-changing trends. Leading Irish designers, including John Rocha, supply A-Wear with a steady stream of clothing.

**BROWN THOMAS** (Grafton St., City Center, tel. 01/679–5666), Dublin's most exclusive department store, stocks the leading designer names in clothing and cosmetics, and lots of stylish accessories. You'll also find clothing by Irish designers.

**CLERY'S** (O'Connell St., North of the Liffey, tel. 01/878–6000), once the city's most fashionable department store, is still worth a visit. You'll find all kinds of merchandise—from fashion to home appliances—on its four floors. Note that goods sold here reflect a distinctly modest, traditional sense of style.

**DUNNES STORES** (St. Stephen's Green Centre, City Center, tel. 01/478–0188; Henry St., North of the Liffey, tel. 01/872–6833; Ilac Shopping Center, Mary St., North of the Liffey, tel. 01/873–0211) is Ireland's largest chain of department stores. All stores stock fashion, household, and grocery items, and have a reputation for value and variety.

**EASON'S** (O'Connell St., North of the Liffey, tel. 01/873–3811; Ilac Shopping Center, Mary St., North of the Liffey, tel. 01/872–1322) is known primarily for its wide variety of books, magazines, and stationery; its larger O'Connell Street branch sells tapes, CDs, records, videos, and other audiovisual goodies.

**MARKS & SPENCER** (Grafton St., City Center, tel. 01/679–7855; Henry St., North of the Liffey, tel. 01/872–8833), perennial competitor to Brown Thomas, stocks everything from fashion (including lingerie) to tasty, unusual groceries. The Grafton Street branch even has its own bureau de change, which doesn't charge commission.

**ROCHES STORES** (Henry St., North of the Liffey, tel. 01/873–0044) is where sensible Dubliners have shopped for generations. Household goods are the specialty, but you'll also find great value on clothes.

## OUTDOOR MARKETS

You'll find a number of open-air markets in Dublin. Outside the city center, weekend markets take place in Blackrock and Dun Laoghaire. **MOORE STREET,** behind the Ilac center, is open Monday–Saturday 9–6. Stalls, which line both sides of the street, sell fruits and vegetables; this is also a good spot to come to buy shoes and boots. Moore Street vendors are known for their sharp wit, so expect the traditional Dublin repartee when you're shopping. You'll find bric-a-brac at the **LIBERTY MARKET** on the north end of Meath Street, open on Friday and Saturday 10–6, Sunday noon–5:30. At the outdoor **MEETING HOUSE SQUARE MARKET,** held Saturday mornings at the heart of Temple Bar, you can buy homemade food stuffs: breads, chocolate, and organic veggies.

# SPECIALTY SHOPS

## Antiques

Dublin is one of Europe's best cities in which to buy antiques, largely due to a long and proud tradition of restoration and high-quality craftsmanship. The Liberties, Dublin's oldest district, is, fittingly, the hub of the antiques trade, and is chock-a-block with shops and traders. Bachelor's Walk, along the quays, also has some decent shops. It's quite a seller's market, but bargains are still possible.

**ANTIQUES AND COLLECTIBLES FAIRS** (tel. 01/670–8295) take place at Newman House (85–86 St. Stephen's Green, City Center) every second Sunday throughout the year.

**CONLON ANTIQUES** (21 Clanbrassil St., Dublin West, tel. 01/453–7323) sells a diverse selection of antiques, from sideboards to fanlights.

**HA'PENNY BRIDGE GALLERIES** (15 Bachelor's Walk, North of the Liffey, tel. 01/872–3950) has four floors of curios, with a particularly large selection of bronzes, silver, and china.

**O'SULLIVAN ANTIQUES** (43–44 Francis St., Dublin West, tel. 01/454–1143 or 01/453–9659) specializes in 18th- and 19th-century furniture and has a high-profile clientele, including Mia Farrow and Liam Neeson.

## Books

You won't have any difficulty weighing down your suitcase with books. Ireland, after all, produced four Nobel literature laureates in just under 75 years. If you're at all interested in modern and contemporary literature, be sure to leave yourself time to browse through the bookstores, as you're likely to find books available here you can't find back home. Best of all, thanks to an enlightened national social policy, there's no tax on books, so if you only buy books, you don't have to worry about getting VAT slips.

**BOOKS UPSTAIRS** (36 College Green, City Center, tel. 01/679–6687) carries an excellent range of special-interest books, including gay and feminist literature, psychology, and self-help books.

**CATHACH BOOKS** (10 Duke St., City Center, tel. 01/671–8676) sells first editions of Irish literature and many other books of Irish interest, plus old maps of Dublin and Ireland.

**DUBLIN BOOKSHOP** (24 Grafton St., City Center, tel. 01/677–5568) is an esteemed, family-owned store that sells mass market books.

**EASON'S/HANNA'S** (29 Nassau St., City Center, tel. 01/677–1255) sells secondhand and mass market paperbacks and hardcovers, and has a good selection of works on travel and Ireland.

**FLYING PIG BOOKSHOP** (17 Crow St., Temple Bar, tel. 01/679–5099) stocks Ireland's largest selection of secondhand science fiction and fantasy books.

**GREENE'S** (Clare St., City Center, tel. 01/676–2544) carries an extensive range of secondhand volumes and new educational and mass market books.

**HODGES FIGGIS** (56–58 Dawson St., City Center, tel. 01/677–4754), Dublin's leading independent, stocks 1½ million books on three floors; there's a pleasant café on the first floor.

**HUGHES & HUGHES** (St. Stephen's Green Centre, City Center, tel. 01/478–3060) has strong travel and Irish-interest sections. There is also a store at Dublin Airport.

**WATERSTONE'S** (7 Dawson St., City Center, tel. 01/679–1415), a large branch of the British chain, features, on two floors, a fine selection of Irish and international books.

**WINDING STAIR** (40 Ormond Quay, North of the Liffey, tel. 01/873–3292) is a charming new- and used-book store overlooking the Liffey. The little upstairs café is the perfect spot for an afternoon of reading.

## China, Crystal, Ceramics, and Jewelry

Ireland is the place to buy Waterford crystal, which is available in a wide range of products, including relatively inexpensive items. Other lines are now gaining recognition, such as Cavan, Galway, and Tipperary crystal. **BROWN THOMAS** is the best department store for crystal; top specialty outlets are listed below.

**BLARNEY WOOLLEN MILLS** (21–23 Nassau St., City Center, tel. 01/671–0068) is one of the best places for Belleek china, Waterford and Galway crystal, and Irish linen.

**CHINA SHOWROOMS** (32/33 Lower Abbey St., North of the Liffey, tel. 01/878–6211), which is more than 60 years old, carries all the top brand names in fine china, including Aynsley, Royal Doulton, and Belleek. It also stocks Waterford, Tyrone, and Tipperary cut hand-cut crystal.

**CRAFTS CENTRE OF IRELAND** (Stephen's Green Centre, City Center, tel. 01/475–4526) carries an impressive inventory of Ireland's most famous contemporary designers, including Michael Kennedy and Diane McCormick (ceramics), Glen Lucas (wood turning), and Jerpoint Glass (glassworks).

**CRANNÓG** (Crown Alley, Temple Bar, tel. 01/671–0805), in Temple Bar, specializes in ceramics and contemporary Irish jewelry, especially silver pendants and rings.

**DESIGNYARD** (E. Essex St., Temple Bar, tel. 01/677–8453) carries beautifully designed Irish and international tableware, lighting, small furniture, and jewelry.

**HOUSE OF IRELAND** (37–38 Nassau St., City Center, tel. 01/671–6133) has an extensive selection of crystal, jewelry, tweeds, sweaters, and other upscale goods.

**KILKENNY SHOP** (5–6 Nassau St., City Center, tel. 01/677–7066) specializes in contemporary Irish-made ceramics, pottery, and silver jewelry, and regularly holds exhibits of exciting new work by Irish craftspeople.

**MCDOWELL** (3 Upper O'Connell St., North of the Liffey, tel. 01/874–4961), a jewelry shop popular with Dubliners, has been in business for more than 100 years.

**TIERNEYS** (St. Stephen's Green Centre, City Center, tel. 01/478–2873) carries a good selection of crystal and china. Claddagh rings, pendants, and brooches are popular.

**WEIR & SONS** (96 Grafton St., City Center, tel. 01/677–9678), Dublin's most prestigious jewelers, sells not only jewelry and watches, but also china, glass, lamps, silver, and leather.

## Museum Stores

**NATIONAL GALLERY OF IRELAND SHOP** (Merrion Sq. W, South of the Liffey, tel. 01/678–5450) has a terrific selection of books on Irish art, plus posters, postcards, note cards, and lots of lovely bibelots.

**NATIONAL MUSEUM SHOP** (Kildare St., South of the Liffey, tel. 01/677–7444 ext. 327) carries jewelry based on ancient Celtic artifacts in the museum collection, contemporary Irish pottery, a large selection of books, and other gift items.

**TRINITY COLLEGE LIBRARY SHOP** (Old Library, Trinity College, City Center, tel. 01/608–2308) sells Irish-theme books, *Book of Kells* souvenirs, and clothing, jewelry, and lovely Irish-made items.

# Music

Irish-recorded material—including traditional folk music, country-and-western, rock, and even a smattering of classical music—is increasingly available in Dublin.

**CELTIC NOTE** (12 Nassau St., City Center, tel. 01/670–4157) is aimed at the tourist market, with a lot of compilations and greatest hits formats.

**CLADDAGH RECORDS** (2 Cecilia St., Temple Bar, tel. 01/679–3664) has a good selection of traditional and folk music.

**GAEL LINN** (26 Merrion Sq., South of the Liffey, tel. 01/676–7283) specializes in traditional Irish-music and Irish-language recordings; it's where the aficionados go.

**HMV** (65 Grafton St., City Center, tel. 01/679–5334; 18 Henry St., North of the Liffey, tel. 01/872–2095) is one of the larger record shops in town.

**MCCULLOGH PIGGOTT** (25 Suffolk St., City Center, tel. 01/677–3138) is the best place in town for instruments, sheet music, scores, and books about music.

**TOWER RECORDS** (6–8 Wicklow St., City Center, tel. 01/671–3250) is the best-stocked international chain.

**VIRGIN MEGASTORE** (14–18 Aston Quay, City Center, tel. 01/677–7361) is Dublin's biggest music store and holds in-store performances by Irish bands.

## Sweaters and Tweeds

Don't think Irish woolens are limited to Aran sweaters and tweed jackets. You'll be pleasantly surprised by the range of hats, gloves, scarves, blankets, and other goods here. If you're traveling outside of Dublin, you may want to wait to make purchases elsewhere, but if Dublin is it, you still have plenty of good shops to choose from. The tweed on sale in Dublin comes

from two main s.
the garments guar...
largest retailers of trad...

**AN TÁIN** (13 Temple Bar S...
carries hyperstylish handma...
accessories.

**BLARNEY WOOLLEN MILLS** (21–23 N...
01/671–0068) carries a good selection ... and
woolen sweaters in all price ranges.

**CLEO LTD.** (18 Kildare St., South of the Liffey, tel. 01/676–1421)
sells hand-knit sweaters and accessories made only from
natural fibers; it also carries its own designs.

**DUBLIN WOOLLEN MILLS** (Metal Bridge Corner, North of the
Liffey, tel. 01/677–5014) at Ha'penny Bridge has a good
selection of hand-knit and other woolen sweaters at competitive
prices.

**KEVIN AND HOWLIN** (31 Nassau St., City Center, tel. 01/677–
0257) specializes in handwoven tweed men's jackets, suits, and
hats, and also sells tweed fabric.

**MONAGHAN'S** (Grafton Arcade, 15–17 Grafton St., City Center,
tel. 01/677–0823) specializes in cashmere.

## Vintage

**FLIP** (4 Upper Fownes St., Temple Bar, tel. 01/671–4299), one of
the original stores in Temple Bar, sells vintage and retro clothing
from the '50s, '60s, and '70s.

**JENNY VANDER** (Georges Street Arcade, City Center, tel. 01/
677–0406) is the most famous name in Irish vintage and retro
clothing. Just browsing through her collection is a pleasure.

## IN THIS CHAPTER

BEACHES 113 • PARTICIPANT SPORTS 114 • Bicycling 114 •
Bowling 114 • Golf 115 • Health Clubs 116 • Horseback
Riding 116 • Jogging 116 • Swimming 117 • Tennis 117 •
SPECTATOR SPORTS 118 • Football 118 • Gaelic Games 118 •
Greyhound Racing 119 • Horse Racing 119 • Rugby 119

*Updated by Muriel Bolger*

# outdoor activities and sports

**HEALTH CLUBS HAVE REALLY CAUGHT ON** in Dublin, and seem to be sprouting up in every corner of the city (especially at hotels). But Dublin has no dearth of opportunities for getting out and moving about. You can explore a beach, horseback-ride, or bike through Phoenix Park, among other options.

## BEACHES

To the north of Dublin city you'll find **NORTH BULL ISLAND**, created over years by the action of the tides. The fine sand here stretches for almost 3 km (2 mi). Bus 130 from Lower Abbey Street stops by the walkway to the beach. **MALAHIDE,** a charming village on the northside DART line, has a clean and easily accessible beach, though the current can be strong. The main beach for swimming on the south side of Dublin is at **KILLINEY** (13 km [8 mi] south of the city center, South County Dublin), a 3-km-long (2-mi-long) shingle (pebbly) beach. The DART train station is right by the beach; get off at Killiney. Near Dublin city center, **SANDYMOUNT STRAND** is a long expanse of fine sand where the tide goes out nearly 3 km (2 mi), but it's not suitable for swimming or bathing because the tide races in so fast. The strand can be reached easily by the DART train.

## PARTICIPANT SPORTS

### Bicycling

Unless you're nutty, don't ride bicycles in the city center—traffic is heavy and most roads don't have shoulders, much less bike lanes. Phoenix Park and some suburbs (especially Ballsbridge, Clontarf, and Sandymount), however, are pleasant once you're off the main roads. You'll find plenty of challenging terrain immediately south of the city, in the Dublin and Wicklow mountains. Don't forget to secure your bicycle if you leave it unattended.

You can rent bicycles for about €57.15 a week; an equivalent amount will be charged for deposit. Nearly 20 companies in the Dublin region rent bicycles; Tourist Information Offices (TIOs) have a full list. **MCDONALD'S** (38 Wexford St., City Center, tel. 01/475–2586) is a centrally located bike repair and rental shop. **MIKE'S BIKE SHOP** (Dun Laoghaire Shopping Center, South County Dublin, tel. 01/280–0417) is a long-established bike outfit in the southside surburbs of Dublin. **TRACKS CYCLES** (8 Botanic Rd., Glasnevin, North County Dublin, tel. 01/873–2455) has an established reputation for being trustworthy in repairs, sales, and rentals of all types of bikes.

### Bowling

Bowling is a popular sport in Dublin; two kinds are played locally. The sedate, exclusive, outdoor variety known as crown-green bowling is played at a number of locations in the suburbs. Dublin also has six indoor 10-pin bowling centers. **HERBERT PARK** (Ballsbridge, South County Dublin, tel. 01/660–1875) has a splendid, baby-soft bowling green. **KENILWORTH BOWLING CLUB** (Grosvenor Sq., South County Dublin, tel. 01/497–2305) welcomes paying visitors, and lessons are available. The green is half the size of a soccer pitch, and smooth as a carpet. **BRAY LEISURE BOWL** (Quinsboro Rd., South County Dublin, tel. 01/286–4455), an indoor bowling center, serves the area near the

Wicklow border. **LEISUREPLEX COOLOCK** (Malahide Rd., North County Dublin, tel. 01/848–5722; Village Green Center, Tallaght, South County Dublin, tel. 01/459–9411) is popular with bowlers from both sides of the city, as it has plenty of lanes and is easy to get to. **METRO BOWL** (149 N. Strand Rd., North County Dublin, tel. 01/855–0400) tends to attract the more serious bowlers. **STILLORGAN BOWL** (Stillorgan, South County Dublin, tel. 01/288–1656) is the oldest 10-pin center in Ireland. **SUPERDOME** (Palmerstown, South County Dublin, tel. 01/626–0700) draws big crowds of teenage and family bowlers.

## Golf

Think idyllic. The Dublin region is a great place for golfers—it has 32 18-hole courses and 16 9-hole courses, and several more 18-hole courses on the way. Below are only some of the major 18-hole courses around Dublin. **DEER PARK** (North County Dublin Howth, tel. 01/832–6039) is a top-quality parkland golf course. **EDMONSTOWN** (South County Dublin Rathfarnham, tel. 01/493–2461), a beautiful golf course, serves an upmarket clientele. **ELM PARK** (South County Dublin Donnybrook, tel. 01/269–3438) welcomes visiting golfers and beginners. **FOXROCK** (Torquay Rd., South County Dublin, tel. 01/289–3992) is a tough golf course with a gorgeous location in the southside suburbs. **HERMITAGE** (North County Dublin Lucan, tel. 01/626–4781) is one of the city's more difficult golf courses. **NEWLANDS** (South County Dublin Clondalkin, tel. 01/459–2903) attracts golfers from the northside of the city. **SUTTON** (South County Dublin Sutton, tel. 01/832–3013) golf course is as exclusive and as pricey as everything else in this wealthy suburb. **WOODBROOK** (South County Dublin Bray, tel. 01/282–4799) is worth the trip out of the city for a day's golf by the sea.

At the **GOLF D2** (Cow St., Temple Bar, tel. 01/672–6181) in Temple Bar you can practice even if it's raining. You strike a real ball with a real club against a huge screen, which tracks the virtual course of your shot. It's a cool idea, and it works. You can play 34 of the world's most famous courses, including St. Andrews and Pebble Beach. It costs €19.05 for a half hour, and you must book ahead.

## Health Clubs

The **IVEAGH FITNESS CLUB** (Christ Church St., Dublin West Dublin 8, tel. 01/454–6555) is next to Christ Church Cathedral, in a complex of beautiful old redbrick buildings. It has a pool, sauna, and full weight room. Just off Grafton Street, the **JACKIE SKELLY FITNESS CENTRE** (41–42 Clarendon St., City Center Dublin 2, tel. 01/677–0040) is perfect if you're staying in a city-center hotel without a gym. In Rathgar village, the **ORWELL CLUB** (75 Orwell Rd, South County Dublin, tel. 01/492–3146) is not far away from many of the southside hotels.

## Horseback Riding

Stables on the outskirts of the city give you immediate access to some excellent riding areas—Counties Dublin, Kildare, Louth, Meath, and Wicklow all have unspoiled country territory. In the city itself, you'll find superb, quiet riding conditions at Phoenix Park, away from the busy main road that bisects the park. About 20 riding stables in the greater Dublin area have horses for hire by the hour or day, both for novices and for experienced riders; a few also operate as equestrian centers and offer lessons. Outside Dublin, **BRITTAS LODGE RIDING STABLES** (Brittas, South County Dublin, tel. 01/458–2726) has fantastic facilities and, wonderfully, is right next to one of the nicest beaches on the East Coast. Horseback riders at the **DEERPARK RIDING CENTER** (Castleknock Rd., Castleknock, North County Dublin, tel. 01/820–7141) canter in Dublin's massive Phoenix Park.

## Jogging

Traffic in Dublin, heavy from early morning until late at night, is getting worse, so if you jog here, expect to dodge vehicles and stop for lights. (Remember *always* to look to your right *and* your left before crossing a street.) If you're staying in Temple Bar or on the western end of the city and you can run 9 km (5½ mi), head to Phoenix Park, easily the nicest place in the city for a jog. If you're on the southside, Merrion Square, St. Stephen's Green, and Trinity College are all good places for short jogs, though be prepared to dodge pedestrians; if you're looking for a longer route, ask your hotel to direct you to the Grand Canal, which has a pleasant path you can run along as far east as the Grand Canal Street Bridge.

## Swimming

One of the best of Dublin's 12 public pools is **TOWNSEND STREET** (Townsend St., City Center, tel. 01/677–0503). **WILLIAMS PARK** (Rathmines, South County Dublin, tel. 01/496–1275) is a quality public pool on the southside. **DUNDRUM FAMILY RECREATION CENTER** (Meadowbrook, Dundrum, South County Dublin, tel. 01/298–4654), a private pool, is open to the public for a small fee. **ST. VINCENT'S** (Navan Rd., North County Dublin, tel. 01/838–4906) is a public pool on the northside of the city. **TERENURE COLLEGE** (Templeogue Rd., South County Dublin, tel. 01/490–7071) is a high school with a pool that's open to the public when school's not in session and competitions aren't taking place. For a hardy dip, there's year-round sea swimming at the **FORTY FOOT BATHING POOL,** a traditional bathing area—in use for more than a century—in Sandycove.

## Tennis

Tennis is one of Dublin's most popular participant sports. Some public parks have excellent tennis facilities open to the public. **BUSHY PARK** (Terenure, South County Dublin, tel. 01/490–0320) has well-maintained public tennis courts. Thanks to its excellent facilities, **HERBERT PARK** (Ballsbridge, South County Dublin, tel. 01/668–4364) attracts some serious tennis players. **ST. ANNE'S PARK** (Dollymount Strand, North County Dublin, tel. 01/833–

8898) has quality tennis courts within sniffing distance of the ocean. **KILTERNAN TENNIS CENTRE** (Kilternan Golf and Country Club Hotel, Kilternan, South County Dublin, tel. 01/295–3729) has everything the tennis player could want—lessons, serving machines, racket stringing—at a price. **LANSDOWNE LAWN TENNIS CLUB** (Londonbridge Rd., South County Dublin, tel. 01/668–0219) is as much about the social gathering as it is about the game itself. Dress appropriately. **WEST WOOD LAWN TENNIS CLUB** (Leopardstown Racecourse, Foxrock, South County Dublin, tel. 01/289–2911) is popular with young, serious-minded players. For more information about playing tennis in Dublin, contact **TENNIS IRELAND** (22 Argyle Sq., Donnybrook, South County Dublin, tel. 01/668–1841).

## SPECTATOR SPORTS

### Football

Soccer—called football in Europe—is very popular in Ireland, largely due to the euphoria resulting from the national team's successes throughout the late 1980s and early 1990s. However, the places where you can watch it aren't ideal—they tend to be small and out-of-date. **LANSDOWNE ROAD,** the vast rugby stadium, is the main center for international matches. League of Ireland matches take place throughout the city every Sunday from September to May. For details, contact the **FOOTBALL ASSOCIATION OF IRELAND** (80 Merrion Sq. S, South of the Liffey, tel. 01/676–6864).

### Gaelic Games

The traditional games of Ireland, Gaelic football and hurling, attract a huge following, with roaring crowds cheering on their county teams. Games are held at Croke Park, the national stadium for Gaelic games, just north of the city center. For details of matches, contact the **GAELIC ATHLETIC ASSOCIATION (GAA)** (Croke Park, North County Dublin, tel. 01/836–3222).

## Greyhound Racing

As elsewhere in the world, greyhound racing is a sport in decline in Ireland. But the track can still be one of the best places to see Dubliners at their most passionate, among friends, and full of wicked humor. **HAROLDS CROSS** (Harolds Cross, South County Dublin, tel. 01/497–1081) is a dilapidated greyhound racing track but serves its purpose. **SHELBOURNE PARK** (Shelbourne Park, South County Dublin, tel. 01/668–3502) is a relatively stylish place to watch greyhound racing. You can book a table in the restaurant that overlooks the track.

## Horse Racing

Horse racing—from flat to hurdle to steeplechase—is one of the great sporting loves of the Irish. The sport is closely followed and betting is popular, but the social side of attending racing is equally important to Dubliners. The main course in Dublin is **LEOPARDSTOWN** (tel. 01/289–3607), an ultramodern course on the southside and home of the Hennessey Gold Cup in February, Ireland's most prestigious steeplechase. **FAIRYHOUSE** (North County Dublin, Co. Meath, tel. 01/825–6167) hosts the Grand National, the most popular steeplechase of the season, every Easter Monday. The **CURRAGH** (tel. 045/441–205), southwest of Dublin, hosts the five Classics, the most important flat races of the season, which are run from May to September. **PUNCHESTOWN** (tel. 045/897–704), outside Naas, County Kildare, is home of the ever-popular Punchestown National Hunt Festival in April.

## Rugby

International rugby matches run during the winter and spring at the vast **LANSDOWNE ROAD STADIUM** (62 Lansdowne Rd., South County Dublin, tel. 01/668–4601). Local matches are also played every weekend during that time. For details about rugby in Ireland, contact the **IRISH RUGBY FOOTBALL UNION** (tel. 01/647–3800, www.irfu.ie/comp/6nats/asp).

## In This Chapter

THE ARTS 122 • Art Galleries 122 • Classical Music
and Opera 124 • Film 124 • Rock and Contemporary
Music 125 • Theater 126 • NIGHTLIFE 127 • Jazz 129 • Pubs 129 •
Gay and Lesbian Pubs 136 • Irish Cabaret 136 • Irish Music
and Dancing 137 • Nightclubs 137

*Updated by Anto Howard*

# nightlife and the arts

**LONG BEFORE STEPHEN DAEDALUS'S EXCURSIONS** into nighttown (read Joyce's *A Portrait of the Artist as a Young Man*), Dublin was proud of its lively after-hours scene, particularly its thriving pubs. Lately, however, with the advent of Irish rock superstars (think U2, the Cranberries, Sinéad O'Connor, Bob Geldof) and the resurgence of Celtic music (think *Riverdance*, the sound track to *Titanic*), the rest of the world seems to have discovered that Dublin is one of the most happening places in the world. Most nights the city's pubs and clubs overflow with young cell phone–toting Dubliners and Europeans who descend on the capital for weekend getaways. The city's 900-plus pubs are its main source of entertainment; many public houses in the city center have live music—from rock to jazz to traditional Irish.

Theater has always been taken seriously in the city that was home to O'Casey, Synge, Yeats, and Beckett. Today Dublin has eight major theaters that reproduce the Irish "classics," and newer fare from the likes of Martin Macdonagh and Conon Macpherson. At long last, the Gaiety Theatre has given long-overlooked opera a home in Dublin. If you're a movie buff, you'll appreciate the two dozen cinema screens in the city center. There are also a number of large, multiscreen cinema complexes in the suburbs, which show current releases made in Ireland and abroad.

The visual arts have always been the poor cousin in the Dublin cultural family. In recent years, small galleries have sprung up all over the city, and the development of Temple Bar Galleries has encouraged a whole new generation of painters, photographers, and sculptors.

Check the following newspapers for informative listings: the *Irish Times* publishes a daily guide to what's happening in Dublin and in the rest of the country, and has complete film and theater schedules. The *Evening Herald* lists theaters, cinemas, and pubs with live entertainment. *In Dublin* and the *Big Issue* are weekly guides to all film, theater, and musical events around the city. You'll find the *Event Guide*, a weekly free paper that lists music, cinema, theater, art shows, and dance clubs, in pubs and cafés around the city. In peak season, consult the free Bord Fáilte leaflet "Events of the Week."

## THE ARTS

### Art Galleries

**THE BRIDGE.** This restored 18th-century Georgian house on the river houses an impressive, open-plan gallery. An internal bridge leads from the gallery shop to the big space at the back where you'll find exhibits of established and rising Irish artists in all media. *6 Upper Ormond Quay, North of the Liffey, tel. 01/872–9702. Mon.–Sat. 10–6, Sun. 2–5.*

**5TH.** This is the gallery every Irish artist wants to be shown in. The location is spectacular: it's on the fifth floor of the impressive Guinness Storehouse. Regularly changing exhibits include painting and sculpture, but there is an emphasis on innovative installation and web art from all over the world. *St. James Gate, Dublin West, tel. 01/408–4800. Daily 9–5:30.*

**GREEN ON RED GALLERIES.** It's strange that this rather unprepossessing gallery, near the back of Trinity College, is one of Dublin's best. Exhibitions are constantly changing—they feature the work of some of the country's—and Britain's—most promising up-and-coming artists. *26–28 Lombard St. E, South of the Liffey, tel. 01/671–3414. Weekdays 11–6, Sat. 11–5.*

**KERLIN GALLERY.** Perhaps Dublin's most important commercial gallery, this large space behind Grafton Street exhibits the work of many of Ireland's important contemporary artists, including such internationally recognized figures as New York–based Sean Scully, Kathy Prendergast, Paul Seawright, and Stephen McKenna. *Anne's La., S. Anne St., City Center, tel. 01/670–9093. Weekdays 10–5:45, Sat. 11–4:30.*

**NATIONAL PHOTOGRAPHIC ARCHIVE.** It's a treasure trove of Irish photographs from the late 19th and early 20th centuries. The Archive also hosts exhibits of work from contemporary Irish photographers—North and South. *Temple Bar, tel. 01/603–0200. Weekdays 10–5, Sat. 10–2.*

**ORIGINAL PRINT GALLERY.** An ultramodern building by the same prominent Dublin architect who designed Temple Bar Gallery, this place specializes in handmade limited editions of prints by Irish artists. Also in the building, the **Black Church Print Studio** (tel. 01/677–3629) exhibits prints. *4 Temple Bar, tel. 01/677–3657. Tues.–Fri. 10:30–5:30, Sat. 11–5, Sun. 2–6.*

**RUBICON GALLERY.** A second-floor gallery overlooking St. Stephen's Green, Rubicon holds a number of yearly exhibitions. They exhibit work in all media. *10 St. Stephen's Green, City Center, tel. 01/670–8055. Mon.–Sat. 11–5:30.*

**SOLOMON GALLERY.** Although not exactly a risk taker, the Solomon has slowly developed a reputation as one of Dublin's leading fine-art galleries. *Powerscourt Townhouse Centre, S. William St., City Center, tel. 01/679–4237. Mon.–Sat. 10–5:30.*

**TEMPLE BAR GALLERY.** At this flagship of the Temple Bar redevelopment project, expect to see the work of emerging Irish photographers, painters, sculptors, and other artists. Shows are on monthly rotating schedules. *5–9 Temple Bar, tel. 01/671–0073. Mon.–Sat. 11–6, Sun. 2–6.*

## Classical Music and Opera

The **BANK OF IRELAND ARTS CENTER** (Foster Pl. S, City Center, tel. 01/671–1488) is great at lunchtime, when classical music and opera recitals take place.

**NATIONAL CONCERT HALL** (Earlsfort Terr., South of the Liffey, tel. 01/475–1666), just off St. Stephen's Green, is Dublin's main theater for classical music of all kinds, from symphonies to chamber groups. It houses the National Symphony Orchestra of Ireland.

**OPERA IRELAND** (John Player House, 276–288 S. Circular Rd., South of the Liffey, tel. 01/453–5519) performs at the Gaiety Theatre; call to find out what's on and when.

**OPERA THEATRE COMPANY** (Temple Bar Music Centre Curved Street, Temple Bar, tel. 01/679–4962) is Ireland's only touring opera company. They perform at venues in Dublin and throughout the country.

**ROYAL HOSPITAL KILMAINHAM** (Military Rd., Dublin West, tel. 01/671–8666) presents frequent classical concerts in its magnificent 17th-century interior.

**ST. STEPHEN'S CHURCH** (Merrion Sq., South of the Liffey, tel. 01/288–0663) stages a regular program of choral and orchestral events under its glorious "pepper canister" cupola.

## Film

**IRISH FILM CENTRE** (6 Eustace St., Temple Bar, tel. 01/677–8788) shows classic and new independent films.

**SAVOY CINEMA** (O'Connell St., North of the Liffey, tel. 01/874–6000), just across from the General Post Office, is a four-screen theater with the largest screen in the country.

**SCREEN CINEMA** (2 Townsend St., City Center, tel. 01/671–4988), between Trinity College and O'Connell Street Bridge, is a popular three-screen art-house cinema.

**UGC MULTIPLEX** (Parnell Center, Parnell St., North of the Liffey, tel. 01/872–8400), a 12-screen theater just off O'Connell Street, is the city center's only multiplex movie house; it shows the latest commercial features.

## Rock and Contemporary Music

The **AMBASSADOR** (1 Parnell Sq., North of the Liffey, tel. 01/889–9403) was once a cinema attached to the Gate Theatre. The plush interior and seats have been removed, and the stripped-down venue now houses visiting bands and "school-disco" nights with music from the '70s and '80s.

**HQ** (57 Middle Abbey St., North of the Liffey, tel. 01/889–9403) is a very comfortable 500-seat venue, located at the Hot Press Irish Music Hall of Fame, that attracts international big-name acts. It's fun to watch performances from the balcony here; there's also a restaurant.

The **INTERNATIONAL BAR** (Wicklow St., City Center, tel. 01/677–9250) has a long-established, tiny, get-close-to-the-band venue upstairs. It hosts theater in the afternoons.

**OLYMPIA THEATRE** (72 Dame St., Temple Bar, tel. 01/677–7744) puts on its "Midnight from the Olympia" shows every Friday and Saturday from midnight to 2 AM, with everything from rock to country.

The **POINT** (Eastlink Br., North of the Liffey, tel. 01/836–3633), a 6,000-capacity arena about 1 km (½ mi) east of the Custom

House on the Liffey, is Dublin's premier venue for internationally renowned acts. Call or send a self-addressed envelope to receive a list of upcoming shows; tickets can be difficult to obtain, so book early.

**TEMPLE BAR MUSIC CENTRE** (Curved St., Temple Bar, tel. 01/ 670–0533) is a music venue, rehearsal space, television studio, and pub rolled into one. It buzzes with activity every day of the week. Live acts range from rock bands to ethnic music to singer-songwriters.

**WHELAN'S** (25 Wexford St., City Center, tel. 01/478–0766), just off the southeastern corner of St. Stephen's Green, is one of the city's best—and most popular—music venues. You'll find well-known performers playing everything from rock to folk to traditional.

## Theater

**ABBEY THEATRE** (Lower Abbey St., North of the Liffey, tel. 01/ 878–7222), the home of Ireland's national theater company, stages mainstream, mostly Irish traditional, plays. Its sister theater at the same address, the **Peacock,** offers more experimental drama. In 1904 W. B. Yeats and his patron, Lady Gregory, opened the theater, which became a major center for the Irish literary renaissance—the place that first staged works by J. M. Synge and Sean O'Casey, among many others. The original theater burned down in 1951, but it reopened with a modern design in 1966.

**ANDREW'S LANE THEATRE** (9–11 Andrew's La., City Center, tel. 01/679–5720) presents experimental productions.

**GAIETY THEATRE** (S. King St., City Center, tel. 01/677–1717) is the home of Opera Ireland when it's not showing musical comedy, drama, and revues.

**GATE THEATRE** (Cavendish Row, Parnell Sq., North of the Liffey, tel. 01/874–4045), an intimate 371-seat theater in a jewel-like Georgian assembly hall, produces the classics and contemporary plays by leading Irish writers.

**NEW PROJECT ARTS CENTRE** (39 E. Essex St., Temple Bar, tel. 01/ 671–2321) is a theater and performance space right in the center of Temple Bar. Fringe and mainstream theater, contemporary music, and experimental art have all found a home here.

**OLYMPIA THEATRE** (72 Dame St., Temple Bar, tel. 01/677–7744) is Dublin's oldest and premier multipurpose theatrical venue. In addition to its high-profile musical performances, it has seasons of comedy, vaudeville, and ballet.

**SAMUEL BECKETT CENTRE** (Trinity College, City Center, tel. 01/ 608–2266) is home to Trinity's Drama Department, as well as visiting groups from around Europe. Dance is often performed here by visiting troupes.

**TIVOLI** (135–138 Francis St., Dublin West, tel. 01/454–4472) brings culture to the heart of old working-class Dublin, the Liberties. Comedy-based shows and the occasional Shakespeare play are favored.

## NIGHTLIFE

Dubliners have always enjoyed a night out, but in the last decade or so they have turned the pleasure into a work of art. The city has undergone a major nightlife revolution and now, for better or worse, bears more than a passing resemblance to Europe's nightclub hotspot, London. Internationally known dance clubs, where style and swagger rule, have replaced the old-fashioned discos, once the only alternative for late-night entertainment. The streets of the city center, once hushed after the pubs had closed, are the scene of what appears to be a never-ending party—you're as likely to find crowds at 2 AM on a Wednesday as you are at the same time on a Saturday. Although the majority of clubs cater to an under-30 crowd of trendy students and young professionals eager to sway to the rhythmic throb of electronic dance music, there are plenty of alternatives, including a number of nightclubs where the dominant sounds range from soul to salsa. While jazz isn't a big part of the nightlife here, a few regular venues do draw the best of local and international talent. And if you're looking for something more mellow, the city doesn't disappoint: there are brasseries, bistros, cafés, and all manner of other late-night eateries where you can sit, sip, and chat until 2 AM or later.

In another trend, some of Dublin's old classic pubs—arguably some of the finest watering holes in the world—have been "reinvented" as popular spots, with modern interiors and designer drinks to attract a younger, upwardly mobile crowd. Beware Dublin Tourism's "Official Dublin Pub Guide 2002," which has a tendency to recommended many of these bland spots. Despite the changes, however, the traditional pub has steadfastly clung to its role as the primary center of Dublin's social life. The city has nearly 1,000 pubs ("licensed tabernacles," writer Flann O'Brien calls them). And while the vision of elderly men enjoying a chin wag over a creamy pint of stout has become something of a rarity, there are still plenty of places where you can enjoy a quiet drink and a chat. Last drinks are called as late as 12:30 AM Monday to Saturday and 11 PM on Sunday; some city-center pubs even have extended opening hours from Thursday through Saturday and don't serve last drinks until 1:45 AM.

A word of warning: although most pubs and clubs are extremely safe, the lads can get lively—public drunkenness is very much a part of Dublin's nightlife. While this is for the most part seen as the Irish form of unwinding after a long week (or, well, day), it can sometimes lead to regrettable incidents (fighting, for instance). In an effort to keep potential trouble at bay, bouncers and security men maintain a visible presence in all clubs and many pubs around the city. At the end of the night, the city center is full of young people trying to get home, which makes for extremely long lines at taxi stands and late-night bus stops, especially on weekends. The combination of drunkenness and impatience can sometimes lead to trouble, so act cautiously. If you need late-night transportation, try to arrange it with your hotel before you go out.

## Jazz

**JJ SMYTH'S** (12 Aungier St., City Center, tel. 01/475–2565) is an old-time jazz venue where Louis Stewart, the granddaddy of Irish jazz, is a regular visitor.

**JURYS BALLSBRIDGE** (Pembroke Rd., Ballsbridge, South of the Liffey, tel. 01/660–5000) attracts the country's top jazz musicians and voices to its lively Sunday evening sessions.

**PENDULUM CLUB** (The Norseman, at Eustace and E. Essex Sts., Temple Bar, tel. 01/671–5135) is the place to go for good jazz. Some of Ireland's top acts play here; internationally recognized musicians occasionally make guest appearances.

## Pubs

### SOUTH CITY CENTER

**BYRNES** (Galloping Green, Stillorgan, South County Dublin, tel. 01/288–7683) has the airy atmosphere of an old-fashioned country pub, even though it's only 8 km (5 mi) from the city center. It's one of the few suburban pubs that haven't been renovated or yuppified.

**DUBLINER PUB** (Jurys hotel, Pembroke Rd., Ballsbridge, South County Dublin, tel. 01/660–5000) has been remade—from a hotel bar—into an old-fashioned Irish pub; it's a busy meeting place at lunch and after work.

**JOHN FALLONS** (129 Dean St., Dublin West), a classy public house in the Liberties, has one of the finest snugs in the city and great photos of old Dublin.

**KIELY'S** (Donnybrook Rd., South County Dublin, tel. 01/283–0208) appears at first glance to be just another modernized pub, but go up the side lane and you'll find a second pub, Ciss Madden's, in the same building. This is an absolutely authentic and convincing reconstruction of an ancient Irish tavern, right down to the glass globe lights and old advertising signs.

**KITTY O'SHEA'S** (Upper Grand Canal St., South of the Liffey, tel. 01/660–9965) has Pre-Raphaelite–style stained glass, lots of sports paraphernalia on the walls, and is popular with sports fans of all types. Its sister pubs are in Brussels and Paris; this is the original.

**O'BRIEN'S** (Sussex Terr., South County Dublin, tel. 01/668–2594), beside the Doyle Burlington hotel, is a little antique gem of a pub, scarcely changed in 50 years, with traditional snugs.

## CITY CENTER

**BRAZEN HEAD** (Bridge St., Dublin West, tel. 01/677–9549), Dublin's oldest pub (the site has been licensed since 1198), has stone walls and open fires—it has hardly changed over the years. The pub is renowned for traditional-music performances and lively sing-along sessions on Sunday evenings. On the south side of the Liffey quays, it's a little difficult to find—turn down Lower Bridge Street and make a right into the old lane.

**CASSIDY'S** (42 Lower Camden St., South of the Liffey, tel. 01/475–1429) is a quiet neighborhood pub with a pint of stout so good that former president Bill Clinton dropped in for one during a visit to Dublin.

The **CELLAR BAR** (24 Upper Merrion St., South of the Liffey, tel. 01/603–0600), at the Merrion Hotel, is located in a stylish 18th-century wine vault, with bare brick walls and vaulted ceilings. It tends to draw a well-heeled crowd.

**CHIEF O'NEILL'S** (Smithfield Village, Dublin West, tel. 01/817–3838), a Dublin hotel, has a large bar-café that's open and airy; it often hosts traditional Irish sessions.

The **COBBLESTONE** (N. King St., Dublin West, tel. 01/872–1799) is a glorious house of ale in the best Dublin tradition. Popular with Smithfield market workers, its chatty imbibers and live traditional music are attracting a wider, younger crowd from all over town.

**DAVY BYRNE'S** (21 Duke St., City Center, tel. 01/671–1298) is a pilgrimage stop for Joyceans. In *Ulysses*, Leopold Bloom stops in here for a glass of burgundy and a Gorgonzola cheese sandwich. He then leaves the pub and walks to Dawson Street, where he helps a blind man cross the road. Unfortunately, the pub is unrecognizable from Joyce's day, but it still serves some fine pub grub.

**DOCKERS** (5 Sir John Rogerson's Quay, South of the Liffey, tel. 01/677–1692), a trendy quayside spot east of city center, is just around the corner from Windmill Lane Studios—where U2 and other noted bands record. At night the area is a little dicey, so come during the day.

**DOHENY & NESBITT** (5 Lower Baggot St., South of the Liffey, tel. 01/676–2945), a traditional spot with snugs, dark wooden furnishings, and smoke-darkened ceilings, has hardly changed over the decades.

**DOYLE'S** (9 College St., City Center, tel. 01/671–0616), a small, cozy pub, is a favorite with journalists from the Irish *Times*, just across the street.

The **GLOBE** (11 S. Great George's St., City Center, tel. 01/671–1220), one of the hippest café-bars in town, draws arty, trendy

Dubliners who sip espresso drinks by day and pack the place at night. There's live jazz on Sunday.

**GROGANS** (15 S. William St., City Center, tel. 01/677–9320), also known as the Castle Lounge, is a small place packed with creative folk.

**HOGAN'S** (35 Great St. George's St., City Center, tel. 01/6677–5904), a huge floor space on two levels, gets jammed most nights, but the old place maintains its style through it all and the beer is top class.

**HORSESHOE BAR** (Shelbourne Méridien Hotel, 27 St. Stephen's Green, City Center, tel. 01/676–6471) is a popular meeting place for Dublin's businesspeople and politicians, though around the semicircular bar there's comparatively little space for drinkers.

**KEHOE'S** (9 S. Anne St., City Center, tel. 01/677–8312) is popular with Trinity students and academics. The tiny back room is cozy.

**MCDAID'S** (3 Harry St., City Center, tel. 01/679–4395) attracted boisterous Brendan Behan and other leading writers in the 1950s; its wild literary reputation still lingers, although the bar has been discreetly modernized and the atmosphere is altogether quieter.

**MODERN GREEN BAR** (31 Wexford St., South of the Liffey, tel. 01/470–0583) offers not only some of Dublin's top DJs but also a wide selection of imported beers. The result: a young, hip crowd who like to dance.

**MOTHER REDCAP'S TAVERN** (Back La., Dublin West, tel. 01/453–8306) is an authentic re-creation of a 17th-century Dublin tavern, with stone walls from an old flour mill, beams, and old prints of the city.

**MULLIGAN'S** (8 Poolbeg St., City Center, tel. 01/677–5582) is synonymous in Dublin with a truly inspirational pint of

# dublin pubs

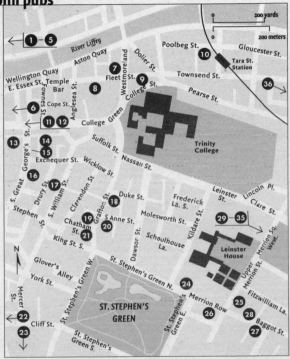

River Liffey

Poolbeg St.
Gloucester St.
Tara St.
Station

Aston Quay
Westmoreland St.
Doller St.
Townsend St.

Wellington Quay
E. Essex St.
Temple Bar
Fleet St.
College St.
Pearse St.

Cope St.
Anglesea St.
College Green

Townes St.

College St.

Trinity
College

Suffolk St.
Nassau St.

S. Great George's St.

Exchequer St.
Wicklow St.

Drury St.
Clarendon St.
Duke St.
Frederick La. S.
Leinster St.
Lincoln Pl.
Clare St.

S. William St.
Grafton St.
S. Anne St.
Molesworth St.
Kildare St.

Chatham St.
Dawson St.
Schoolhouse La.
Leinster House

Stephen

King St. S.

N

Glover's Alley

York St.

Mercer St.

Cliff St.

St. Stephen's Green W.
St. Stephen's Green N.

ST. STEPHEN'S
GREEN

St. Stephen's Green E.

Merrion Row

Upper Merrion St.
Merrion Sq. West

Fitzwilliam La.

Baggot St.

St. Stephen's
Green S.

Brazen Head, 6
Byrnes, 29
Cassidy's, 23
The Cellar Bar, 25
Chief O'Neill's, 4
Cobblestone, 23
Davy Byrne's, 18
Dockers, 36
Doheny & Nesbitt, 28
Doyle's, 9

Dubliner Pub, 30
The Front Lounge, 12
The George, 13
The Globe, 15
Grogans, 17
GUBU, 3
Hogan's, 16
Horseshoe Bar, 24
John Fallons, 35

Johnnie Fox's, 31
Kehoe's, 20
Kiely's, 32
Kitty O'Shea's, 33
McDaid's, 19
Modern Green Bar, 22
Mother Redcap's Tavern, 11
Mulligan's, 10
Neary's, 21

O'Brien's, 34
O'Donoghue's, 26
Oliver St. John Gogarty, 8
Out on the Liffey, 1
Palace Bar, 7
Ryan's Pub, 2
Stag's Head, 14
Toner's, 27

Guinness. Until a few years ago no women were admitted. Today journalists, locals, and students of both genders flock here for the perfect pint.

**NEARY'S** (1 Chatham St., City Center, tel. 01/677–7371), with an exotic Victorian-style interior, was once the haunt of music-hall artists and a certain literary set, including Brendan Behan. Join the actors from the adjacent Gaiety Theatre for a good pub lunch.

**O'DONOGHUE'S** (15 Merrion Row, South of the Liffey, tel. 01/676–2807), a cheerful, smoky hangout, has impromptu musical performances that often spill out onto the street.

**THE OLD STAND** (37 Exchequer St., South of the Liffey, tel. 01/677–7220), one of the oldest pubs in the city, is named after the old stand at Landsdowne Road, home to Irish Rugby and Soccer. The place is renowned for great pints and fine steaks.

**RYAN'S PUB** (28 Parkgate St., Dublin West, tel. 01/677–6097) is one of Dublin's last genuine, late-Victorian-era pubs, and has changed little since its last (1896) remodeling.

**STAG'S HEAD** (1 Dame Ct., City Center, tel. 01/679–3701) dates from 1770 and was rebuilt in 1895; theater people from the nearby Olympia, journalists, and Trinity students turn up around the unusual counter, fashioned from Connemara red marble.

**TONER'S** (139 Lower Baggot St., South of the Liffey, tel. 01/676–3090), though billed as a Victorian bar, actually goes back 200 years, with an original flagstone floor to prove its antiquity, as well as wooden drawers running up to the ceiling—a relic of the days when bars doubled as grocery shops. Oliver St. John Gogarty accompanied W. B. Yeats here, in what was purportedly the latter's only visit to a pub.

## COUNTY DUBLIN—SOUTHSIDE

**JOHNNIE FOX'S** (South County Dublin Glencullen, Co. Dublin, tel. 01/295–5647), 12 km (8 mi) from the city center, sits 1,000 ft up in the Dublin Mountains, making it the highest licensed premises in Ireland. You approach it by a winding and steeply climbing road that turns off the main Dublin–Enniskerry road at Stepaside. Refusing to bow to the whims of modernization, it has steadfastly maintained its traditional character—oak tables, rough-stone floor flags strewn with sawdust, and ancient bric-a-brac, including copper kettles, crockery, old prints, and guns—and appears very much as it did in the early 19th century, when Daniel O'Connell used it as a safe house for his seditious meetings. You can get lunch and dinner here; the specialty is seafood, and it alone is worth the journey. In the evenings expect to hear traditional Irish music.

### TEMPLE BAR

The **FRONT LOUNGE** (33 Parliament St., Temple Bar, tel. 01/679–3988), a modern pub, caters to a mixed crowd of young professionals, both gay and straight.

**OLIVER ST. JOHN GOGARTY** (57 Fleet St., Temple Bar, tel. 01/671–1822) is a lively bar that attracts all ages and nationalities, and which overflows in summer. On most nights there is traditional Irish music upstairs.

**PALACE BAR** (21 Fleet St., Temple Bar, tel. 01/677–9290), scarcely changed over the past 60 years, is tiled and rather barren looking, but is popular with journalists and writers. (The Irish Times is nearby.) The walls are hung with cartoons drawn by the illustrators who used to spend time here.

**THE PORTERHOUSE** (16–18 Parliament St., Temple Bar, tel. 01/679–8847) is one of the few bars in Ireland that brews its own beer. The Plain Porter won the best stout at the "Brewing Oscars" beating out the mighty Guinness. The tasteful interior is all dark woods and soft lighting.

## Gay and Lesbian Pubs

The **GEORGE** (89 S. Great George's St., City Center, tel. 01/478–2983), Dublin's two-floor main gay pub, draws an almost entirely male crowd; its nightclub stays open until 2:30 AM nightly except Tuesday. The "alternative bingo night," with star drag act Miss Shirley Temple Bar, is a riot of risqué fun.

**GUBU** (Capel St., North of the Liffey, tel. 01/874–0710) is the newest venture north of the river by the hugely successful owners of the Globe. It draws a mixed crowd. The pool table downstairs is a bonus.

**OUT ON THE LIFFEY** (27 Ormond Quay, Dublin West, tel. 01/872–2480) is Dublin's second gay pub; it draws a mixed gay and straight crowd—both men and women.

## Irish Cabaret

### BALLSBRIDGE/SOUTH CITY CENTER
**DOYLE BURLINGTON HOTEL** (Upper Leeson St., South of the Liffey, tel. 01/660–5222) has a high-class lounge featuring a well-performed Irish cabaret—with dancing, music, and song.

**JURYS HOTEL** (Pembroke Rd., Ballsbridge, South of the Liffey, tel. 01/660–5000) stages a traditional Irish cabaret.

### CITY CENTER
**CASTLE INN** (Christ Church Pl., Dublin West, tel. 01/475–1122) is really just a huge pub that has traditional Irish music and dancing with dinner in a medieval-style banquet hall.

### COUNTY DUBLIN—NORTHSIDE
**ABBEY TAVERN** (North County Dublin Howth, tel. 01/839–0307) has a rip-roaring cabaret with rousing traditional Irish songs.

**CLONTARF CASTLE** (Castle Ave., North County Dublin Clontarf, tel. 01/833–2321) is a spectacular setting for a traditional night of song and comedy.

# Irish Music and Dancing

## SOUTH DUBLIN

**COMHALTAS CEOLTÓIRI ÉIREANN** (35 Belgrave Sq., South County Dublin Monkstown, tel. 01/280–0295) is the place to come for a boisterous summer evening of Irish music and dancing.

**HARCOURT HOTEL** (Harcourt St., South of the Liffey, tel. 01/478–3677) is where some of the best traditional musicians gather for wild jam sessions.

# Nightclubs

The dominant sound in Dublin's nightclubs is electronic dance music, and the crowd that flocks to them every night of the week is of the trendy, under-25 generation. At a few pubs, however, you're more likely to hear tango than techno—such as the weekend nightclub at the Gaiety Theatre, Thursday night at the Pod, and Sunday night at Lillie's Bordello.

## CITY CENTER

**LEESON STREET**—just off St. Stephen's Green, south of the Liffey, and known as "the strip"—is a main nightclub area that starts at pub closing time and lasts until 4 AM. It has lost its gloss since the turn of the millennium, however, as a number of lap-dancing establishments have opened. The dress code at Leeson Street's dance clubs is informal, but jeans and sneakers are not welcome. Most of these clubs are licensed only to sell wine, and the prices can be exorbitant (up to €26 for a mediocre bottle); the upside is that most don't charge to get in.

**LILLIE'S BORDELLO** (Grafton St., City Center, tel. 01/679–9204) is a popular spot for a trendy, professional crowd, as well as for rock and film stars. On Sunday night, the strict dress code—shirt and jacket, no trainers, no jeans (unless you're famous)—is relaxed for a night of live music and DJs.

The **POD** (Harcourt St., South of the Liffey, tel. 01/478–0166), also known as the "Place of Dance," qualifies as Dublin's most-renowned dance club, especially among the younger set. Whether you get in depends as much on what you're wearing as on your age. It helps to look stylish or rich, except on Thursday night, when the club hosts a no-frills, no-nonsense night of dance-floor jazz and funk.

The **RED BOX** (Old Harcourt St. Station, Harcourt St., South of the Liffey, tel. 01/478–0166), adjacent to the Pod and the Chocolate Bar, can pack in more than 1,000 people and surround them with state-of-the-art sound and light. It regularly hosts Irish and international rock acts, and celebrity DJs from Europe and the United States. It has full bar facilities.

At **RENARDS** (St. Fredrick St., South of the Liffey, tel. 01/677–5876) you'll find thirtysomethings who like to let their hair down. The music can be a bit predictable; the jazz-and-supper-club is a better option.

**RÍ RA** (Dame Ct., City Center, tel. 01/677–4835) is part of the hugely popular Globe bar. The name means "uproar" in Irish, and on most nights the place does go a little wild. It's one of the best spots in Dublin for fun, no-frills dancing. Upstairs is more low-key.

## TEMPLE BAR

The **KITCHEN** (E. Essex St., Temple Bar, tel. 01/677–6359) is in the basement of the Clarence hotel. Its popularity, mainly with an under-30s crowd, owes much to its owners, Bono and the Edge of U2.

**VIPER ROOM** (5 Aston Quay, Temple Bar, tel. 01/672–5566), decorated in rich reds and purples, is a delightfully decadent late-night club that plays funky, chart, and rhythm n' blues. Downstairs you'll find live jazz and salsa.

## Not a Night Owl?

You can learn a lot about a place if you take its pulse after dark. So even if you're the original early-to-bed type, there's every reason to vary your routine when you're away from home.

**EXPERIENCE THE FAMILIAR IN A NEW PLACE** Whether your thing is going to the movies or going to concerts, it's always different away from home. In clubs, new faces and new sounds add up to a different scene. Or you may catch movies you'd never see at home.

**TRY SOMETHING NEW** Do something you've never done before. It's another way to dip into the local scene. A simple suggestion: Go out later than usual—go dancing late and finish up with breakfast at dawn.

**DO SOMETHING OFFBEAT** Look into lectures and readings as well as author appearances in book stores. You may even meet your favorite novelist.

**EXPLORE A DAYTIME NEIGHBORHOOD AT NIGHT** Take a nighttime walk through an explorable area you've already seen by day. You'll get a whole different view of it.

**ASK AROUND** If you strike up a conversation with like-minded people during the course of your day, ask them about their favorite spots. Your hotel concierge is another resource.

**DON'T WING IT** As soon as you've nailed down your travel dates, look into local publications or surf the Net to see what's on the calendar while you're in town. Look for hot regional acts, dance and theater, big-name performing artists, expositions, and sporting events. Then call or click to order tickets.

**CHECK OUT THE NEIGHBORHOOD** Whenever you don't know the neighborhood you'll be visiting, review safety issues with people in your hotel. What's the transportation situation? Can you walk there, or do you need a cab? Is there anything else you need to know?

**CASH OR CREDIT?** Know before you go. It's always fun to be surprised—but not when you can't cover your check.

## IN THIS CHAPTER

CITY CENTER (Southside) 142 • TEMPLE BAR 147 • SOUTH
CITY CENTER—BALLSBRIDGE 149 • CITY CENTER
(Northside) 154 • SOUTH COUNTY DUBLIN SUBURBS 157 •
DUBLIN AIRPORT 158

*Updated by Anto Howard*

# where to stay

**"AN ABSOLUTE AVALANCHE OF NEW HOTELS"** is how the *Irish Times* characterized Dublin's hotel boom. New lodgings have sprung up all over the city, including the much-talked-about Chief O'Neill's in Smithfield, and a few in Ballsbridge, an inner "suburb" that's a 20-minute walk from the city center. Demand for rooms means that rates are still high at the best hotels by the standards of any major European or North American city (and factoring in the exchange rate means a hotel room can take a substantial bite out of any traveler's budget). The recent slump in tourist travel, however, has caused a few hotels to cut their prices considerably. Service charges range from 15% in expensive hotels to zero in moderate and inexpensive ones. Be sure to inquire when you make reservations.

Many hotels have a weekend, or "B&B," rate that's often 30%–40% cheaper than the ordinary rate; some hotels also have a midweek special that provides discounts of up to 35%. These rates are available throughout the year but are harder to get in high season. Ask about them when booking a room (they are available only on a prebooked basis), especially if you plan a brief or weekend stay. If you've rented a car and you're not staying at a hotel with secure parking facilities, it's worth considering a location out of the city center, such as Dalkey or Killiney, where the surroundings are more pleasant and you won't have to worry about parking on city streets.

Dublin has a decent selection of less-expensive accommodations— including many moderately priced hotels with basic but agreeable rooms. As a general rule of thumb, lodgings on the north side of the river tend to be more affordable than those on the south. Many B&Bs, long the mainstay of the economy end of the market, have upgraded their facilities and now provide rooms with private bathrooms or showers, as well as multichannel color televisions and direct-dial telephones, for around €46 a night per person. B&Bs tend to be in suburban areas—generally a 15-minute bus ride from the center of the city. This is not in itself a great drawback, and savings can be significant.

Assume that hotels operate on the **European Plan** (EP, with no meals) unless we specify otherwise.

| CATEGORY | COST* |
|---|---|
| $$$$ | over €280 |
| $$$ | €230–€280 |
| $$ | €178–€230 |
| $ | under €178 |

*All prices are for two people in a double room, including VAT and a service charge (often applied in larger hotels).*

## CITY CENTER (SOUTHSIDE)

$$$$ **CONRAD DUBLIN INTERNATIONAL.** In a seven-story redbrick and smoked-glass building just off St. Stephen's Green, the Conrad, owned by the Hilton Group, firmly aims for international business travelers. Gleaming, light marble graces the large, formal lobby. Rooms are rather cramped and have uninspiring views of the adjacent office buildings, but are nicely outfitted with natural wood furnishings, painted in sand colors and pastel greens, and have Spanish marble in the bathrooms. A note to light sleepers: the air-conditioning/heating system can be noisy. The hotel has two restaurants: the informal Plurabelle and the plusher Alexandra Room. *Earlsfort Terr., South of the Liffey, tel. 01/676–5555, fax 01/676–5424, www.conradinternational.ie. 182 rooms with bath, 9 suites. 2 restaurants, room service, in-room data ports, in-room safes, minibars,*

*cable TV, in-room VCRs, gym, bar, concierge, business services, meeting rooms, free parking; no-smoking rooms, no-smoking floor. AE, DC, MC, V.*

**$$$$** **FITZWILLIAM HOTEL.** It has been dubbed a "designer" hotel for its impeccable decor: everything from light fixtures to luggage racks to staff uniforms is smartly designed. The modern glass building has a large roof garden and overlooks St. Stephen's Green. The spacious rooms are furnished in a contemporary, comfortable style. Conrad Gallagher, one of Ireland's most acclaimed chefs, presides over the rooftop restaurant. *St. Stephen's Green, City Center, tel. 01/ 478–7000, fax 01/478–7878, www.fitzwilliamh.com. 128 rooms with bath, 2 suites. Restaurant, room service, cable TV, in-room VCRs, in-room data ports, gym, bar, laundry service, business services, meeting rooms; no-smoking rooms. AE, DC, MC, V.*

**$$$$** **LE MÉRIDIEN SHELBOURNE.** Paris has the Ritz, New York has the
★ Plaza, and Dublin has the Shelbourne. Waterford chandeliers, gleaming old masters on the wall, and Irish Chippendale chairs invite you to linger in the lobby. Each guest room has fine, carefully selected furniture and luxurious drapes, with splendid antiques in the older rooms. Those in front overlook St. Stephen's Green, but rooms in the back, without a view, are quieter. The Lord Mayor's Lounge, off the lobby, is a perfect rendezvous spot and offers a lovely afternoon tea—a real Dublin tradition. *27 St. Stephen's Green, City Center, tel. 01/663–4500; 800/543–4300 in the U.S., fax 01/661–6006, www.shelbourne.ie. 181 rooms with bath, 9 suites. 2 restaurants, room service, indoor pool, health club, hot tub, sauna, 2 bars, free parking; no-smoking rooms. AE, DC, MC, V.*

**$$$$** **MERRION.** The home of the Duke of Wellington, hero of the
★ Battle of Waterloo, is one of the four exactingly restored Georgian town houses that make up this luxurious hotel. The stately rooms are appointed in classic Georgian style—from the crisp linen sheets to the Carrara marble bathrooms. Some are vaulted with delicate Adamesque plasterwork ceilings, and others are graced with magnificent, original marble fireplaces. Rooms in the old house are more expensive than those in the new extension. You

know this place must be special, because leading Dublin restaurateur Patrick Guilbaud has moved his eponymous restaurant here. *Upper Merrion St., South of the Liffey, tel. 01/603–0600, fax 01/603–0700, www.merrionhotel.com. 225 rooms with bath, 45 suites. 2 restaurants, room service, in-room data ports, in-room safes, minibars, cable TV, in-room VCRs, indoor pool, hair salon, massage, steam room, 2 bars, dry cleaning, laundry service, concierge, business services, meeting rooms, free parking; no-smoking rooms, no-smoking floor. AE, DC, MC, V.*

**$$$$ WESTBURY.** This comfortable, modern hotel is in the heart of southside Dublin, right off the city's buzzing shopping mecca: Grafton Street. Join elegantly dressed Dubliners for afternoon tea in the spacious mezzanine-level main lobby, which is furnished with antiques. Alas, the utilitarian rooms—painted in pastels—don't share the lobby's elegance. More inviting are the suites, which combine European stylings with tasteful Japanese screens and prints. The flowery Russell Room serves formal lunches and dinners; the downstairs Sandbank, a seafood restaurant and bar, looks like a turn-of-the-20th-century establishment. *Grafton St., City Center, tel. 01/679–1122, fax 01/679–7078, www.jurysdoyle.com. 204 rooms with bath, 8 suites. 2 restaurants, room service, minibars, cable TV, in-room VCRs, bar, dry cleaning, laundry service, free parking; no-smoking rooms. AE, DC, MC, V.*

**$$$ DAVENPORT.** The gorgeous, bright-yellow neoclassic facade of this hotel behind Trinity College was originally built in the 1860s to front a church. Tasteful, deep colors and functional furnishings characterize the reasonably spacious rooms and larger suites. The hotel restaurant, Lanyon's, serves breakfast, lunch, and dinner amid traditional Georgian surroundings. In the comfortable President's Bar, see how many heads of state you can identify in the photos covering the walls. *Merrion Sq., South of the Liffey, tel. 01/661–6800; 800/327–0200 in the U.S., fax 01/661–5663, www.ocallaghanhotels.ie. 118 rooms with bath, 2 suites. Restaurant, room service, minibars, cable TV, in-room VCRs, bar, dry cleaning, laundry* *service, concierge, business services, meeting rooms, free parking; no-smoking rooms. AE, DC, MC, V.*

**$$–$$$ WESTIN DUBLIN.** Reconstructed from three 19th-century landmark buildings across the road from Trinity College, the Westin is all about location. The public spaces re-create a little of the splendor of yesteryear: marble pillars, tall mahogany doorways, blazing fireplaces, and period detailing on the walls and ceilings. The bedrooms, on the other hand, are functional and small, with the crisp, white Indian linen and custom-made beds the only luxurious touches. The rooms that overlook Trinity are a little more expensive, but the engaging view makes all the difference. *College Green, South of the Liffey, tel. 01/645–1000, fax 01/645–1234, www.westin.com. 141 rooms with bath, 22 suites. Restaurant, room service, minibars, cable TV, 2 bars, dry cleaning, laundry service, concierge, business services, meeting rooms, free parking; no-smoking rooms. AE, DC, MC, V.*

**$$ CLARION STEPHEN'S HALL HOTEL & SUITES.** Dublin's only all-suites hotel occupies a tastefully modernized Georgian town house just off Stephen's Green. The suites, considerably larger than the average hotel room, include one or two bedrooms, a separate sitting room, a fully equipped kitchen, and bath. They are comfortably equipped with quality modern furniture. Top-floor suites have spectacular city views, and ground-floor suites have private entrances. Morel's Restaurant serves breakfast, lunch, and dinner. *14–17 Lower Leeson St., South of the Liffey, tel. 01/661–0585, fax 01/661–0606, www.premgroup.ie. 34 suites. Restaurant, room service, cable TV, 2 bars, meeting rooms, free parking; no-smoking rooms. AE, DC, MC, V.*

**$–$$ DRURY COURT HOTEL.** This small hotel, a two-minute walk from Grafton Street, is just around the corner from some of the city's best restaurants. Rooms are done in subtle greens, golds, and burgundies. In the parquet-floored rathskeller dining room you can get breakfast and dinner; lunch is served in the casual Digges Lane Bar, frequented by many young Dubliners. *28–30 Lower Stephens St., City Center, tel. 01/475–1988, fax 01/478–5730,* *www.indigo.ie/~ druryct/. 30 rooms with bath, 2 suites. Restaurant, room service, bar, dry cleaning, laundry service, meeting room. AE, DC, MC, V.*

**$–$$  NUMBER 31.** Two Georgian mews strikingly renovated in the early '60s as the private home of Sam Stephenson, Ireland's leading modern architect, are now connected via a small garden to the grand town house they once served. Together they form a marvelous guest house a short walk from St. Stephen's Green. Owners Deirdre and Noel Comer serve made-to-order breakfasts at refectory tables in the balcony dining room. The white-tiled sunken living room, with its black leather sectional sofa and modern artwork that includes a David Hockney print, will make you think you're in California. *31 Leeson Close, South of the Liffey, tel. 01/676–5011, fax 01/676–2929, www.number31.ie. 21 rooms with bath. Dry cleaning, laundry service, free parking; no-smoking rooms. AE, MC, V.*

**$  AVALON HOUSE.** Many young, independent travelers rate this cleverly restored redbrick Victorian building the most appealing of Dublin's hostels. A 2-minute walk from Grafton Street and 5–10 minutes from some of the city's best music venues, the hostel has a mix of dormitories, rooms without bath, and rooms with bath. The dorm rooms and en-suite quads all have loft areas that offer more privacy than you'd typically find in a multibed room. The Avalon Café serves food until 10 PM but is open as a common room after hours. *55 Aungier St., City Center, tel. 01/475–0001, fax 01/475–0303, www.avalon-house.ie. 35 4-bed rooms with bath, 5 4-bed rooms without bath, 4 twin rooms with bath, 4 single rooms without bath, 22 twin rooms without bath, 5 12-bed dorms, 1 10-bed dorm, 1 26-bed dorm. Café, bar; no room TVs. AE, MC, V.*

**$  CENTRAL HOTEL.** Established in 1887, this grand, old-style redbrick hotel is in the heart of the city center, steps from Grafton Street, Temple Bar, and Dublin Castle. Rooms are small but have high ceilings and practical but tasteful furniture. Adjacent to the hotel is Molly Malone's Tavern, a lively hotel-bar with plenty of regulars who come for the atmosphere and the live, traditional

Irish music on Friday and Saturday nights. The restaurant and Library Bar—one of the best spots in the city for a quiet pint— are on the first floor. 1–5 Exchequer St., City Center, tel. 01/679–7302, fax 01/679–7303, www.centralhotel.ie. 67 rooms with bath, 3 suites. Restaurant, room service, 2 bars, dry cleaning, laundry service, concierge, business services, meeting rooms. AE, DC, MC, V.

**$ JURYS CHRISTCHURCH INN.** Expect few frills at this functional budget hotel, part of a Jurys minichain that offers a low, fixed room rate for up to three adults or two adults and two children. (The **Jurys Custom House Inn** [Custom House Quay, South of the Liffey Dublin 1, tel. 01/607–5000, fax 01/829–0400], at the International Financial Services Centre, operates according to the same plan.) The biggest plus is the pleasant location, facing Christ Church Cathedral and within walking distance of most city-center attractions. The rather spartan rooms are decorated in pastel colors and utilitarian furniture. Christ Church Pl., Dublin West, tel. 01/454 0000, fax 01/454–0012, www.jurysdoyle.com. 182 rooms with bath. Restaurant, bar, parking (fee); no-smoking rooms. AE, DC, MC, V.

**$ KILRONAN HOUSE.** A five-minute walk from St. Stephen's Green, this large, late-19th-century terraced house with a white facade has been carefully converted into a guest house. The furnishings are updated each year. Richly patterned wallpaper and carpets decorate the guest rooms, and orthopedic beds (rather rare in Dublin hotels, let alone guest houses) help to guarantee a restful night's sleep. 70 Adelaide Rd., South of the Liffey, tel. 01/475–5266, fax 01/478–2841, www.dublinn.com. 15 rooms with bath. Free parking; no-smoking room. MC, V.

## TEMPLE BAR

**$$$$ THE CLARENCE.** You might well bump into celebrity friends of co-owners Bono and the Edge of U2 at this contemporary hotel, understated to the point of austerity. The Octagon Bar and the Tea Room Restaurant are popular Temple Bar watering holes. Guest rooms are decorated in a mishmash of earth tones accented with deep purple, gold, cardinal red, and royal blue. With the exception of those in the penthouse suite, rooms are small. The laissez-faire service seems to take its cue from the minimalist style, so if you like to be pampered, stay elsewhere. *6–8 Wellington Quay, Temple Bar,* tel. *01/407–0800,* fax *01/407–0820, www.theclarence.ie. 47 rooms with bath, 3 suites. Restaurant, minibars, cable TV, bar, dry cleaning, laundry service, meeting rooms, free parking; no-smoking rooms. AE, DC, MC, V.*

**$–$$ PARLIAMENT.** Although the Parliament is in one of Dublin's finest Edwardian buildings, its interior is very much functional, if tidy, and appeals to mainly a business clientele—drawn by the location near the Central Bank and Trinity College. Rooms are a good size, with a simple, slightly monotonous beige and off-white color scheme. The Senate Restaurant and Forum Bar keep up the democratic theme with reliable selections. *Lord Edward St., Temple Bar,* tel. *01/670–8777,* fax *01/670–8787, www.regencyhotels.com. 63 rooms with bath. Restaurant, bar, cable TV; no-smoking rooms. AE, DC, MC, V.*

**$–$$ TEMPLE BAR.** The hotel's delightful Art Deco lobby has a large, old-fashioned cast-iron fireplace, natural-wood furniture, and lots of plants. Off the lobby are a small cocktail bar and the bright, airy, glass-roofed Terrace Restaurant, which serves sandwiches, pastas, omelets, and fish all day. Mahogany furnishings and autumn green and rust colors characterize the guest rooms, nearly all of which have double beds (this makes them more than a little cramped). The Boomerang nightclub on the premises is open both to guests and the public. The hotel is in a former bank building, around the corner from Trinity College. *Fleet St., Temple Bar,* tel. *01/677–3333,* fax *01/677–3088, www.towerhotelgroup.ie/templebar. 133 rooms with bath, 2 suites. Restaurant, cable TV, 2 bars, nightclub, parking (fee). AE, DC, MC, V.*

**$ PARAMOUNT.** At the heart of modern Temple Bar, this medium-size hotel has opted to maintain its classy Victorian facade. The foyer continues this theme of solid elegance, with incredibly comfortable leather couches, bleached-blond oak floors, and Burgundy red curtains. The bedrooms are decorated in dark woods and subtle colors—very 1930s (you just know if Bogart and Bacall ever came to Dublin they'd have to stay here). If you're fond of a tipple, try the hotel's Art Deco Turks Head Bar and Chop House. *Parliament St. and Essex Gate, Temple Bar, tel. 01/417–9900, fax 01/417–9904, www.paramounthotel.ie. 70 rooms with bath. Restaurant, cable TV, in-room data ports, bar, laundry service; no-smoking rooms. AE, DC, MC, V.*

## SOUTH CITY CENTER—BALLSBRIDGE

**$$$$ BERKELEY COURT.** The most quietly elegant of Dublin's large modern hotels, Berkeley Court has a glass-and-concrete exterior that's designed in a modern, blocklike style, and is surrounded by verdant grounds. The vast white-tiled and plushly carpeted lobby has roomy sofas and antique planters. The large rooms are decorated in golds, yellows, and greens, with antiques or reproductions of period furniture; bathrooms are tiled in marble. There are five luxury suites. The Berkeley Room restaurant has table d'hôte and à la carte menus; the more informal Conservatory Grill, with large windows, serves grilled food and snacks. *Lansdowne Rd., South County Dublin, tel. 01/660–1711; 800/550–0000 in the U.S., fax 01/661–7238, www.jurysdoyle.com. 158 rooms with bath, 29 suites. 2 restaurants, room service, cable TV, gym, hair salon, some hot tubs, bar, shops, dry cleaning, laundry service, business services, meeting rooms, free parking; no-smoking rooms. AE, DC, MC, V.*

**$$$$ FOUR SEASONS.** Much controversy surrounds the brash, postmodern architecture of this hotel. The six-floor building mixes a Victorian and Georgian design with modern glass and concrete. The impressive landscaping makes the hotel seem like an oasis; a big effort has been made to ensure that a bit of greenery can be seen from most rooms. Rooms are spacious, with large windows that allow the light to flood in. A selection of landscapes on the walls gives the place a more human feel. *Simmonscourt Rd., South County Dublin, tel. 01/665–4000, fax 01/665–4099, www.fourseasons.com.*

192 rooms with bath, 67 suites. Restaurant, cable TV, coffee shop, indoor pool, hot tub, bar, shop, dry cleaning, laundry service, business services, meeting rooms, free parking; no-smoking rooms. AE, DC, MC, V.

$$$$ **HERBERT PARK HOTEL.** Adjacent to a park of the same name, and beside the River Dodder, the hotel's large lobby has floor-to-ceiling windows and a slanted glass roof. The spacious bar, terrace lounge, and restaurant are Japanese-inspired minimalist in style. Relaxing shades of blue and cream predominate in the nicely sized rooms; all have individually controlled air-conditioning, a large desk, and two telephone lines. Some look onto the park. Two of the suites have large balconies with views of the park or the leafy suburbs. The restaurant has a terrace where you can dine in warm weather. *Ballsbridge, South County Dublin, tel. 01/667–2200, fax 01/ 667–2595, www.herbertparkhotel.ie. 150 rooms with bath, 3 suites. Restaurant, cable TV, gym, bar, business services, free parking; no-smoking rooms. AE, DC, MC, V.*

$$$$ **JURYS BALLSBRIDGE AND THE TOWERS.** These adjoining seven-story hotels, popular with businesspeople, have more atmosphere than most comparable modern hotels. The Towers has an edge over its older, larger, less-expensive companion, Jurys Ballsbridge. The Towers' rooms are decorated in blue and gold with built-in, natural-wood furniture; the large beds and armchairs are comfortable. Jurys Ballsbridge, on the other hand, has large, plainly decorated rooms with light walls and brown drapes; furnishings are functional but uninspired. *Jurys Ballsbridge: Pembroke Rd.; The Towers: Lansdowne Rd., Ballsbridge, South County Dublin, tel. 01/660–5000, fax 01/679–7078, www.jurysdoyle.com. Jurys Ballsbridge: 300 rooms with bath, 3 suites; the Towers: 100 rooms with bath, 4 suites with kitchenettes. 2 restaurants, coffee shop, indoor-outdoor pool, hot tub, bar, cabaret (May–Oct.), shop, dry cleaning, laundry service, business services, meeting rooms, free parking. AE, DC, MC, V.*

$$$ **DOYLE BURLINGTON.** In high contrast to the hotel's impersonal, 1972 glass-and-concrete facade, the staff are friendly and attentive. Public rooms, especially the large bar, have mahogany counters

and hanging plants that enhance the conservatory-style setting. The generous-size rooms, in the usual modern minimalism (neutral tones), have large picture windows. At night, Annabel's nightclub and the seasonal (summer) Irish cabaret are both lively spots. The Burlington has no sports and health facilities but the Doyle hotel group, which runs it, has an arrangement that allows you to use the RiverView Sports Club in nearby Clonskeagh for €6.35 a visit. *Upper Leeson St., South County Dublin, tel. 01/660–5222, fax 01/660–8496, www.jurysdoyle.com. 523 rooms with bath. 2 restaurants, room service, cable TV, 3 bars, cabaret (May–Oct.), nightclub, shops, dry cleaning, laundry service, business services, meeting rooms, free parking; no-smoking room. AE, DC, MC, V.*

**$$–$$$** ★ **HIBERNIAN.** This early 20th-century Edwardian nurses' home designed by Albert E. Murray—one of the architects of the Rotunda Hospital—is now a small luxury hotel. One of the city's most elegant and intimate hotels, it retains the distinctive red-and-amber brick facade and has smallish rooms, nicely done in pastels, with deep-pile carpets and comfortable furniture. The public rooms, in cheerful chintz and stripes, include a period-style library and a sun lounge—both comfortable spaces to relax before or after a dinner in the hotel's intimate restaurant, the Patrick Kavanagh Room. Amid all this Victorian elegance, the owners haven't forgotten the warming touches. *Eastmoreland Pl. off Upper Baggot St., South County Dublin, tel. 01/668–7666 or 800/414243, fax 01/660–2655, www.hibernianhotel.com. 40 rooms with bath. Restaurant, bar, parking (fee). AE, DC, MC, V.*

**$–$$** **MOUNT HERBERT HOTEL.** The Loughran family's sprawling accommodation includes a number of large, Victorian-era houses. It overlooks some of Ballsbridge's fine rear gardens and is right near the main rugby stadium; the nearby DART will have you in the city center in seven minutes. The simple rooms are painted in light shades and contain little besides beds; all have bathrooms and 10-channel TVs. The lounge is a good place to relax. The restaurant, which overlooks the English-style back garden (floodlit

# dublin lodging

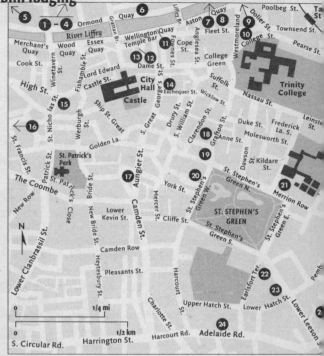

Ariel Guest House, 38

Arlington Hotel, 7

Avalon House, 17

Berkeley Court, 36

Bewleys at Newlands Cross, 16

Central Hotel, 14

Charleville Lodge, 4

Chief O'Neill's, 5

The Clarence, 11

Clarion Hotel IFSC, 29

Clarion Stephen's Hall Hotel & Suites, 23

Conrad Dublin International, 22

Davenport, 27

Doyle Burlington, 30

Drury Court Hotel, 19

Fitzpatrick Castle Dublin, 40

Fitzwilliam Hotel, 20

Four Seasons, 33

Globetrotters Tourist Hotel, 28

Great Southern Hotel, 3

Herbert Park Hotel, 34

Hibernian, 31

Holiday Inn Dublin Airport, 2

153

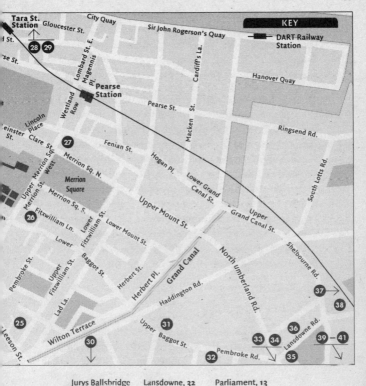

Jurys Ballsbridge
and the
Towers, 35

Jurys
Christchurch
Inn, 15

Jurys Skylon, 1

Jurys Tara, 39

Kilronan
House, 24

Lansdowne, 32

Le Méridien
Shelbourne , 22

Merrion, 26

The Morrison, 6

Mount
Herbert Hotel, 37

Number 31, 25

Paramount, 12

Parliament, 13

Royal Dublin
Hotel, 9

Royal Marine, 41

Temple Bar, 8

Westbury, 18

Westin Dublin, 10

at night) and children's play area, serves three meals a day; at dinner you can get steaks and stews. 7 Herbert Rd., South County Dublin, tel. 01/668–4321, fax 01/660–7077, www.mountherberthotel.ie. 200 rooms with bath. Restaurant, cable TV, sauna, bar, shop, business services, meeting rooms, free parking; no-smoking rooms. AE, DC, MC, V.

**$ ★ ARIEL GUEST HOUSE.** This redbrick 1850 Victorian guest house in a tree-lined suburb is one of Dublin's finest, just a few steps from a DART stop and a 15-minute walk from St. Stephen's Green. Restored rooms in the main house are lovingly decorated with Victorian and Georgian antiques, Victoriana, and period wallpaper and drapes. The 13 rooms at the back of the house are more spartan, but all are immaculate. A Waterford-crystal chandelier hangs over the comfortable leather and mahogany furniture in the gracious, fireplace-warmed drawing room. Owner Michael O'Brien is an extraordinarily helpful and gracious host. 52 Lansdowne Rd., South County Dublin, tel. 01/668–5512, fax 01/668–5845, www.ariel-house.com. 40 rooms with bath. Free parking. MC, V.

**$ ★ LANSDOWNE.** The cozy, Georgian-style rooms in this small Ballsbridge hotel have delightful floral-pattern furnishings. Photos of sports personalities hang on the walls of the Green Blazer bar in the basement, a popular haunt for local businesspeople and fans of the international rugby matches held at nearby Lansdowne Road; you can get a bite to eat here all day. Next to the bar is Parker's Restaurant, which specializes in seafood and grilled steaks. 27 Pembroke Rd., South County Dublin, tel. 01/668–2522, fax 01/668–5585, www.lansdownehotel.com. 38 rooms with bath, 2 suites. Restaurant, bar, free parking. AE, DC, MC, V.

## CITY CENTER (NORTHSIDE)

**$$$$ THE MORRISON.** Halfway between the Ha'penny and Capel Street bridges, it's no more than a 10-min walk to Trinity College. The highly modern interior—designed by John Rocha, Ireland's most acclaimed fashion designer—can be a bit cold. He had the last word on everything down to the toiletries and staff uniforms.

Rooms have unfussy modern furnishings and are high-tech, with top-of-the-line entertainment units, satellite TV, and ISDN lines. The Halo restaurant has an Asian fusion theme. *Ormond Quay, North of the Liffey, tel. 01/887–2400, fax 01/878–3185, www.morrisonhotel.ie. 88 rooms with bath, 7 suites. 2 restaurants, room service, in-room data ports, minibars, cable TV, in-room VCRs, 2 bars, dry cleaning, laundry service, concierge, business services, meeting rooms, free parking; no-smoking rooms. AE, DC, MC, V.*

**$$–$$$ CHIEF O'NEILL'S.** Named after a 19th-century Corkman who became chief of police in Chicago, this hotel is by far the largest building in Smithfield Village. Smallish, high-tech rooms all have ISDN lines and look thoroughly up-to-date —with chrome fixtures and minimalist furnishings. Top-floor suites have delightful roof-top gardens with views of the city on both sides of the Liffey. The café-bar has live traditional music and contemporary Irish food, and Asian cuisine is available in Kelly & Ping, a bright, airy restaurant off Duck Lane, a shopping arcade that's part of the hotel complex. *Smithfield Village, North of the Liffey, tel. 01/817–3838, fax 01/817–3839, www.chiefoneills.com. 70 rooms with bath, 3 suites. Restaurant, room service, in-room data ports, minibars, cable TV, in-room VCRs, gym, bar, shops, dry cleaning, laundry service, free parking; no-smoking rooms. AE, DC, MC, V.*

**$$–$$$ CLARION HOTEL IFSC.** Smack in the middle of the International Financial Services Centre, the Clarion—with an office-block-like exterior—is indistinguishable from many of the financial institutions that surround it. The public spaces are bright and cheery, if a little uninspired, and the bedrooms are all straight lines and contemporary light-oak furnishings. Shades of blue and taupe create a calm environment. Try get a room at the front with great views out over the Liffey. They mainly cater to the business traveller, so weekend bargains are a definite possibility—make sure you ask for them. *IFSC, North of the Liffey, tel. 01/433–8800, fax 01/433–8811, www.clarionhotelifsc.com. 147 rooms with bath, 13 suites. Restaurant, room service, in-room data ports, minibars, cable TV,* indoor pool, gym, health club, massage, bar, dry cleaning, laundry service, free parking; no-smoking rooms. AE, DC, MC, V.

**$$ ROYAL DUBLIN HOTEL.** O'Connell Street is not what it once was, but this renovated, upmarket hotel has just about a perfect location at the top of the old thoroughfare. All of the northside's major attractions are nearby, and you can walk south to Trinity College in 10 minutes. The public spaces are well-lit, and decorated in glass and brass. Rooms are spacious, and the hotel has built a solid reputation for extra-friendly service. The Georgian Room and Raffles bar try to put on posh English airs (think crisp linen), but the casual warmth of the staff undoes the stuffiness. *O'Connell St., North of the Liffey, tel. 01/873–3666, fax 01/873–3120, www. royaldublin.com. 117 rooms with bath, 3 suites. Restaurant, room service, in-room data ports, minibars, cable TV, in-room VCRs, bar, dry cleaning, laundry service; no-smoking rooms. AE, MC, V.*

**$–$$ ARLINGTON HOTEL.** A converted auction house on the quays is the setting for this privately owned boutique hotel. The rooms have a Georgian style, with soothing pastel yellow or lavender walls; spreads and drapes are awash in golds, rusts, and blues, and have patterns and details evocative of tapestries. The bar, boisterous and echo-filled, is more mead hall than cozy pub. Rich upholstery, romantic lighting, and hearty Irish fare (full breakfast is included in the rates) make the restaurant more intimate, however. The hotel has limited off-street parking. *23–25 Bachelor's Walk, O'Connell Bridge, North of the Liffey, tel. 01/804–9100, fax 01/804–9112, www.arlington.ie. 115 rooms with bath, 6 suites. Restaurant, cable TV, in-room data ports, bar, dance club, baby-sitting, laundry service, meeting rooms, free parking; no-smoking rooms. AE, DC, MC, V.*

**$ CHARLEVILLE LODGE.** It's worth the short commute to the city center (the No. 10 bus takes five minutes and it's a great walk in good weather) to enjoy the luxury (and great-value) of the Charleville Lodge. It's part of a row of beautifully restored Victorian terraced houses in the historic Phibsborough area of Dublin's northside. The dramatically lit residents' lounge, with a working fireplace, is a great spot to chat with other travelers who have dared to stray off the beaten path. Rooms are brightly colored and spacious. *268–272 N. Circular Rd., North of the Liffey, tel. 01/838–6633, fax 01/838–5854, www.charlevillelodge.ie. 30 rooms with bath. Free parking; no-smoking rooms. MC, V.*

**$ GLOBETROTTERS TOURIST HOSTEL.** Globetrotters is a giant step up from many Dublin hostels, with a pleasant outdoor courtyard; clean, locking dorm rooms with en-suite showers; a turf fire; comfortable bunk beds (with lamps for late-night reading); and a delicious all-you-can-eat breakfast. Plus, you're within walking distance of the city center, one block from the bus station, and two blocks from the train station. They also own the Town House, a cute bed-and-breakfast in the same building. *46 Lower Gardiner St., North County Dublin, tel. 01/873–5893, fax 01/878–8787, www.townhouse.ie. 94 dorm beds, 38 double rooms with bath. Restaurant. MC, V.*

## SOUTH COUNTY DUBLIN SUBURBS

**$$–$$$ ROYAL MARINE.** This 1870 seaside hotel has comfortable, capacious rooms with contemporary furnishings. The lofty ceilings from the original building are preserved in the suites, with four-poster beds and sitting rooms. Ask for a room at the front of the hotel, facing Dun Laoghaire harbor. *Marine Rd., South County Dublin, Dun Laoghaire, tel. 01/280–1911, fax 01/280–1089, www.ryan-hotel.com. 95 rooms with bath, 8 suites. Restaurant, room service, 2 bars, business services, free parking; no-smoking rooms. AE, DC, MC, V.*

**$$ FITZPATRICK CASTLE DUBLIN.** For its sweeping views over Dun
★ Laoghaire and Dublin Bay, the Fitzpatrick is worth the 15-km (9-mi) drive from the city center. The original part of the hotel is an 18th-century stone castle, with a substantial modern addition housing rooms; many are furnished with antiques and four-poster beds, and have large bathrooms. The hotel is convenient to golfing, horseback riding, and fishing; the fitness facilities include an 82-ft heated pool. The views from Killiney Hill, behind the hotel, are spectacular; the seaside village of Dalkey and Killiney

Beach are both within walking distance. *South County Dublin Killiney, tel. 01/230–5400, fax 01/230–5466, www.fitzpatricks.com. 113 rooms with bath. Restaurant, cable TV, indoor pool, health club, bar, meeting rooms, free parking. AE, DC, MC, V.*

**$ BEWLEYS AT NEWLANDS CROSS.** Stay at this four-story hotel on the southwest outskirts of the city if you're planning to head out of the city early (especially to points in the Southwest and West) and don't want to deal with morning traffic. The hotel is emulating the formula popularized by Jurys Inns, in which rooms—here each has a double bed, a single bed, and a sofa bed—are a flat rate for up to three adults or two adults and two children. *Newlands Cross, Naas Rd., South County Dublin, tel. 01/464–0140, fax 01/464–0900, www.bewleyshotels.com. 256 rooms with bath. Café, free parking; no-smoking rooms. AE, MC, V.*

**$ JURYS TARA.** On the main coast road 10–15 minutes from the Dun Laoghaire ferry terminal and 6½ km (4 mi) from the city center, you'll find this unpretentious, informal seven-story hotel. It's also near the Booterstown Marsh Bird Sanctuary. The best rooms are in the original section and face Dublin Bay; rooms in the addition have slightly more modern furnishings. The restaurant serves grilled fish, steaks, and omelets. The hotel staff is very personable. *Merrion Rd., South County Dublin, tel. 01/269–4666, fax 01/269–1027, www.jurysdoyle.com. 114 rooms with bath. Restaurant, bar, dry cleaning, laundry service, free parking; no-smoking rooms. AE, DC, MC, V.*

## DUBLIN AIRPORT

**$$–$$$ HOLIDAY INN DUBLIN AIRPORT.** You'll find basic but spacious rooms at the Holiday Inn, a low-rise redbrick structure with a plain exterior. The Bistro Restaurant serves both fish and meat entrées and vegetarian dishes; Sampans serves Chinese cuisine at dinner only. There's live music in the bar on weekends. Guests have access to a nearby health club. *Dublin Airport, North County Dublin, tel. 01/808–0500, fax 01/844–6002, www.forte-hotels.com. 250 rooms* with bath. 2 restaurants, room service, bar, free parking; no-smoking rooms. AE, DC, MC, V.

**$ GREAT SOUTHERN HOTEL.** Within the airport complex, near the main terminal, and next to the main road into the city center you'll find a modern five-story hotel that's part of one of Ireland's most respected chains. The accommodation itself is spacious and comfortable, if a little unexciting, but the service is exceptional. *Dublin Airport, North County Dublin, tel. 01/844–6000, fax 01/844–6001, www.dubairport.gsh.ie. 147 rooms with bath. Restaurant, room service, bar, free parking. AE, DC, MC, V.*

**$ JURYS SKYLON.** On the main road into Dublin city center from the airport is a modern five-story hotel with a concrete-and-glass facade and generous-size rooms, plainly decorated in cool pastels. Rooms have double beds and a pair of easy chairs are almost the only furniture. A glass-fronted lobby with a large bar and the Rendezvous Room restaurant dominate the public areas. The cooking is adequate but uninspired, with dishes such as grilled steak, poached cod, and omelets. *Upper Drumcondra Rd., North County Dublin, tel. 01/837–9121, fax 01/837–2778, www.jurysdoyle.com. 88 rooms with bath. Restaurant, bar, free parking. AE, DC, MC, V.*

# practical information

## Air Travel to and from Dublin

### CARRIERS

Aer Lingus is the national flag carrier of Ireland, with regularly scheduled flights to Dublin from New York's JFK, Boston's Logan, Chicago's O'Hare, and LAX. Delta has a daily departure from Atlanta that flies first to Shannon and on to Dublin. Continental flies daily direct to Dublin, departing from Newark Airport in New Jersey. With the exception of special offers, the prices of the four airlines tend to be similar.

From the United Kingdom, six airlines now serve destinations in Ireland: Aer Lingus, Ryanair, City Jet, Go, British Airways, and British Midland Airways. Aer Lingus operates 12 flights from Heathrow and Gatwick Airports. British Airways has a regular schedule out of Heathrow. British Midland operates 10 flights to Dublin from Heathrow. Ryanair operates several no-frills, low-price flights from Luton and Stanstead airports. City Jet flies from the very central London City Airport. Go flies from Edinburgh. Ryanair is known for being the cheapest, but this means cutting back on comfort and services.

Major European carriers, such as Air France, Lufthansa, Sabena, SAS, and Alitalia, run direct services to Dublin from most European capital cities and major regional airports, especially those in Germany.

Aer Lingus provides service around Ireland to Dublin, Cork, Galway, Kerry, and Shannon. Aer Arann Express, which used to run only an island-hopping service, has recently expanded into the domestic market, flying from Dublin to Cork, Derry, Donegal, Galway, Knock, and Sligo. British Airways also offers daily flights from Dublin to Derry.

➤**AIRLINES AND CONTACTS: Aer Lingus** (tel. 01/844–4747 in Dublin; 800/474–74247 in the U.S. and Canada; 0845/973–7747 or 020/8899–4747 in the U.K.; 02/9244–2123 in Australia; 09/308–3351 in New Zealand, www.aerlingus.com). **British Airways** (tel. 800/626–747 in Dublin; 0845/773–3377 in the U.K., www.britishairways.com). **British Midlands** (tel. 01/283–8833 in Dublin; 0870/607–0555 in the U.K., www.britishmidland.co.uk). **City Jet** (tel. 01/844–5566 in Dublin). **Continental** (tel. 1890/925–252 in Ireland; 800/231–0856 in the U.S., www.continental.com). **Delta** (tel. 01/844–4166 or 01/676–8080 in Dublin; 800/241–4141 in the U.S. and Canada, www.delta.com). **Go** (tel. 1890/923–922 in Ireland). **Ryanair** (tel. 01/844–4411 in Dublin; 08701/569–569 in the U.K., www.ryanair.com).

## Airports and Transfers

Dublin Airport, 10 km (6 mi) north of the city center, serves international and domestic airlines.

➤**AIRPORT INFORMATION: Dublin Airport** (tel. 01/844–4900).

### AIRPORT TRANSFERS

Dublin Bus operates a shuttle service between Dublin Airport and the city center with departures outside the arrivals gateway; pay the driver inside the coach. The single fare is €4.50. Service runs from 5:45 AM to 11:30 PM, at intervals of about 20 minutes (after 8 PM buses run every hour), to as far as Dublin's main bus station (Busaras), behind the Custom House on the northside. Journey time from the airport to the city center is normally 30 minutes, but it may be longer in heavy traffic. If you have time take a regular bus for €1.30.

A taxi is a quicker alternative than the bus to get from the airport to Dublin center. A line of taxis waits by the arrivals gateway; the fare for the 30-minute journey to any of the main city-center hotels is about €15.25 to €17.80 plus tip (tips don't have to be large but they are increasingly expected). Ask about the fare before leaving the airport.

➤**TAXIS AND SHUTTLES: Busaras** (tel. 01/830–2222). **Dublin Bus** (tel. 01/873–4222).

## Bus Travel to and from Dublin

Busaras is Dublin's main bus station, just behind the Custom House on the northside.

Numerous bus services run between Britain and the Irish Republic, but **be ready for long hours on the road and possible delays.** All buses to the Republic use either the Holyhead–Dublin or Fishguard/Pembroke–Rosslare ferry routes. National Express, a consortium of bus companies, has Supabus (as its buses are known) services from all major British cities to more than 90 Irish destinations. Slattery's, an Irish company, has services from London, Manchester, Liverpool, Oxford, Birmingham, Leeds, and North Wales to more than 100 Irish destinations.

➤**BUS INFORMATION: Busaras** (tel. 01/830–2222). **Bus Éireann** (tel. 01/836–6111 in the Republic of Ireland, www.buseireann.ie). **National Express** (tel. 08705/808–080 in the U.K., www.nationalexpress.co.uk). **Slattery's** (tel. 020/7482–1604 in the U.K.). **Ulsterbus** (tel. 028/9033–3000 in Northern Ireland, www.ulsterbus.co.uk).

## Bus Travel Within Dublin

Dublin has an extensive network of buses, most of which are green double-deckers. Some bus services run on cross-city routes, including the smaller "Imp" buses, but most buses start in the city center. Buses to the north of the city begin in the Lower Abbey Street–Parnell Street area, while those to the west begin in Middle Abbey Street and in the Aston Quay area. Routes to the southern suburbs begin at Eden Quay and in the College Street area. A number of services are links to DART stations, and another regular bus route connects the two main provincial railway stations, Connolly and Heuston. If the destination board indicates AN LÁR, that means that the bus is going to the city center. Late-night buses run Monday to Saturday to 3 AM on all major routes; the fare is €3.80.

Museumlink is a shuttle service that links up the Natural History Museum, National Museum, and Collins Barracks. You can catch it outside any of the three museums.

### FARES AND SCHEDULES

Timetables (€3.20) are available from Dublin Bus, staffed weekdays 9–5:30, Saturday 9–1. Fares begin at 55p and are paid to the driver, who will accept inexact fares, but you'll have to go to the central office in Dublin to pick up your change as marked on your ticket. Change transactions and the city's heavy traffic can slow service down considerably.

➤BUS INFORMATION: Dublin Bus (59 Upper O'Connell St., North of the Liffey, tel. 01/873–4222).

## Business Hours

Banks are open 10–4, Monday–Friday. They remain open until 5 one afternoon per week; the day of week varies, although it's usually Thursday. Post offices are open weekdays 9–5 and Saturdays 9–1. Museums and sights are generally open Tuesday–Saturday 10–5 and Sunday 2–5.

## Car Rental

➤**MAJOR AGENCIES: Alamo** (tel. 800/522–9696; 020/8759–6200 in the U.K.; www.alamo.com). **Avis** (tel. 800/331–1084; 800/879–2847 in Canada; 02/9353–9000 in Australia; 09/526–2847 in New Zealand; 0870/606–0100 in the U.K.; www.avis.com). **Budget** (tel. 800/527–0700; 0870/156–5656 in the U.K.; www.budget.com). **Dollar** (tel. 800/800–6000; 0124/622–0111 in the U.K., where it's affiliated with Sixt; 02/9223–1444 in Australia; www.dollar.com). **Hertz** (tel. 800/654–3001; 800/263–0600 in Canada; 020/8897–2072 in the U.K.; 02/9669–2444 in Australia; 09/256–8690 in New Zealand; www.hertz.com). **National Car Rental** (tel. 800/227–7368; 020/8680–4800 in the U.K.; www.nationalcar.com).

### INSURANCE

When driving a rented car you are generally responsible for any damage to or loss of the vehicle. Before you rent, see what coverage your personal auto-insurance policy and credit cards provide.

Before you buy collision coverage, check your existing policies—you may already be covered. However, collision policies that car-rental companies sell for European rentals usually do not include stolen-vehicle coverage.

### REQUIREMENTS AND RESTRICTIONS

In Ireland your own driver's license is acceptable. An International Driver's Permit is a good idea; it's available from the American or Canadian Automobile Association and, in the United Kingdom, from the Automobile Association or Royal Automobile Club. These international permits are universally recognized, and having one in your wallet may save you a problem with the local authorities.

Most rental companies require you to be over 23 to rent a car in Ireland (a few will rent to those over 21) and to have had a license for more than a year. Some companies also refuse to rent to visitors over 70.

## Car Travel

Traffic in Ireland has increased exponentially in the last few years, and nowhere has the impact been felt more than in Dublin, where the city's complicated one-way streets are congested not only during the morning and evening rush hours but often during much of the day. If possible, avoid driving a car except to get in and out of the city (and be sure to ask your hotel or guest house for clear directions to get you out of town).

Traffic signs are the same as in the rest of Europe, and roadway markings are standard. Note that a continuous white line down the center of the road prohibits passing. Barred markings on the road and flashing yellow beacons indicate a crossing, where pedestrians have right of way. At a junction of two roads of equal importance, the driver to the right has right of way.

### EMERGENCY SERVICES

Membership in a breakdown service is definitely advisable if you're using your own car in Ireland. The Automobile Association of Ireland is a sister organization of its English counterpart and is highly recommended.

➤CONTACTS: **Automobile Association of Ireland** (tel. 01/ 617–9999, www.aaireland.ie).

### RULES OF THE ROAD

The Irish, like the British, **drive on the left-hand side of the road.** Safety belts must be worn by the driver and all passengers, and children under 12 must travel in the back unless riding in a car seat. It is compulsory for motorcyclists and their passengers to wear helmets.

Drunk-driving laws are strict. The legal limit is 80 mg of alcohol per 100 ml of blood. Ireland has a Breathalyzer test, which the police can administer anytime. If you refuse to take it, the odds are you'll be prosecuted anyway. As always, the best advice is **don't drink if you plan to drive.**

## Children in Dublin

The Irish go to great lengths to make children welcome. Many hotels offer baby-sitting services, and most will supply a cot if given advance notice. Hotel and pub restaurants often have a children's menu and can supply a high chair if necessary. Unlike in Great Britain, Irish licensing laws allow children under 14 into pubs—although they may not consume alcohol on the premises until they are 18, and they are expected to leave by about 5:30 PM (although they may be allowed to stay until 7 PM, depending on how busy the pub gets). This is a boon if you are touring by car, because pubs are perfect for lunch or tea stops.

While most attractions and bus and rail journeys offer a rate of half price or less for children, **look for "family tickets,"** which may be cheaper and usually cover two adults and up to four children. The Irish Tourist Board (Bord Fáilte) publishes "A Tour of Favorite Kids' Places," which covers a week's worth of sights around the country.

Be sure to plan ahead and **involve your youngsters** as you outline your trip. When packing, include things to keep them busy en route. On sightseeing days try to schedule activities of special interest to your children. Places that are especially appealing to children are indicated by a rubber duckie icon (☺) in the margin.

A sampling of theater productions for children can also be found at local playhouses around the country. Listings of upcoming events are published in the **Irish Times** (€1.27) each Wednesday.

If you are renting a car, don't forget to **arrange for a car seat** when you reserve. For general advice about traveling with children, consult *Fodor's FYI: Travel with Your Baby* (available in bookstores everywhere).

## Computers on the Road

### INTERNET CAFÉS

In the city center are a number of Internet cafés, which all charge between €3.50 and €7 an hour. Betacafe serves coffee and sandwiches. Cyberia is very popular with students, who tend to spend hours playing computer games. Planet Cyber Café is the city's best, with top-notch computers and a good coffee bar. You'll find some of the cheapest places on Thomas Street, as it's not smack in the center of town.

➤**ADDRESSES: Betacafe** (Arthouse, Curved St., Temple Bar, tel. 01/671–5717). **Cyberia** (The Granary, Temple La. S, Temple Bar, tel. 01/679–7607). **Planet Cyber Café** (13 Andrews St., City Center, tel. 01/670–5182).

## Consumer Protection

Whenever shopping or buying travel services in Ireland, **pay with a major credit card,** if possible, so you can cancel payment or get reimbursed if there's a problem. If you're doing business with a particular company for the first time, **contact your local Better Business Bureau and the attorney general's offices** in your state and (for U.S. businesses) the company's home state as well. Have any complaints been filed? Finally, if you're buying a package or tour, always **consider travel insurance** that includes default coverage (☞ Insurance).

➤**BBBS: Council of Better Business Bureaus** (4200 Wilson Blvd., Suite 800, Arlington, VA 22203, tel. 703/276–0100, fax 703/525–8277, www.bbb.org).

## Customs and Duties

When shopping, **keep receipts** for all purchases. Upon reentering the country, **be ready to show customs officials what you've bought**. If you feel a duty is incorrect or object to the way your clearance was handled, note the inspector's badge number and ask to see a supervisor. If the problem isn't resolved, write to the appropriate authorities, beginning with the port director at your point of entry.

### IN AUSTRALIA

Australian residents who are 18 or older may bring home $A400 worth of souvenirs and gifts (including jewelry), 250 cigarettes or 250 grams of tobacco, and 1,125 ml of alcohol (including wine, beer, and spirits). Residents under 18 may bring back $A200 worth of goods. Prohibited items include meat products. Seeds, plants, and fruits need to be declared upon arrival.

➤INFORMATION: **Australian Customs Service** (Regional Director, Box 8, Sydney, NSW 2001, Australia, tel. 02/9213–2000 or 1300/363263; 1800/020504 quarantine-inquiry line, fax 02/9213–4000, www.customs.gov.au).

### IN CANADA

Canadian residents who have been out of Canada for at least seven days may bring home C$500 worth of goods duty-free. If you've been away fewer than seven days but more than 48 hours, the duty-free allowance drops to C$200; if your trip lasts 24–48 hours, the allowance is C$50. You may not pool allowances with family members. Goods claimed under the C$500 exemption may follow you by mail; those claimed under the lesser exemptions must accompany you. Alcohol and tobacco products may be included in the seven-day and 48-hour exemptions but not in the 24-hour exemption. If you meet the age requirements of the province or territory through which you reenter Canada, you may bring in, duty-free, 1.14 liters (40 imperial ounces) of wine or liquor or 24 12-ounce cans or bottles of beer or ale. If you are 16 or older you may bring in, duty-free, 200 cigarettes and 50 cigars. Check ahead of time with Revenue Canada or the Department of Agriculture for policies regarding meat products, seeds, plants, and fruits.

You may send an unlimited number of gifts worth up to C$60 each duty-free to Canada. Label the package UNSOLICITED GIFT—VALUE UNDER $60. Alcohol and tobacco are excluded.

➤INFORMATION: Canada Customs and Revenue Agency (2265 St. Laurent Blvd. S, Ottawa, Ontario K1G 4K3, Canada, tel. 204/983–3500, 506/636–5064, 800/461–9999, www.ccra-adrc.gc.ca/).

## IN IRELAND

Clearing customs at major gateway airports is a fairly quick and easy procedure. Duty-free allowances have been abolished for those traveling between countries in the European Union (Austria, Belgium, Denmark, Finland, France, Germany, Greece, Ireland, Italy, Luxembourg, the Netherlands, Portugal, Spain [but not the Canary Islands], Sweden, the United Kingdom, but not the Channel Islands or Gibraltar).

For goods purchased outside the EU, you may import duty-free: (1) 200 cigarettes or 100 cigarillos or 50 cigars or 250 grams of smoking tobacco; (2) 2 liters of wine, and either 1 liter of alcoholic drink over 22% volume or 2 liters of alcoholic drink under 22% volume (sparkling or fortified wine included); (3) 50 grams (60 mls) of perfume and ¼ liter of toilet water; and (4) other goods (including beer) to a value of €180.30 per person (€92.70 per person for travelers under 15 years of age).

Goods that cannot be freely imported to the Irish Republic include firearms, ammunition, explosives, illegal drugs, indecent or obscene books and pictures, oral smokeless tobacco products, meat and meat products, poultry and poultry products, plants and plant products (including shrubs, vegetables, fruit, bulbs, and seeds), meat and meat products, and hay or straw even used as packing. Domestic cats and dogs from outside the United Kingdom and live animals from outside Northern Ireland must be quarantined for six months.

No animals or pets of any kind may be brought into Northern Ireland without a six-month quarantine. Other items that may not be imported include fresh meats, plants and vegetables, controlled drugs, and firearms and ammunition.

➤INFORMATION: Customs and Excise (Irish Life Building, 2nd floor, Middle Abbey St., Dublin 1, tel. 01/878–8811, www.revenue.ie).

## IN NEW ZEALAND
Homeward-bound residents 17 or older may bring back $700 worth of souvenirs and gifts. Your duty-free allowance also includes 4.5 liters of wine or beer; one 1,125-ml bottle of spirits; and either 200 cigarettes, 250 grams of tobacco, 50 cigars, or a combination of the three up to 250 grams. Prohibited items include meat products, seeds, plants, and fruits.

➤INFORMATION: New Zealand Customs (Head office: The Custom House, 17–21 Whitmore St., Box 2218, Wellington, tel. 09/300–5399 or 0800/428–786, www.customs.govt.nz).

## IN THE U.K.
If you are a U.K. resident and your journey was wholly within the European Union (EU), you won't have to pass through customs when you return to the United Kingdom. If you plan to bring back large quantities of alcohol or tobacco, check EU limits beforehand. In most cases, if you bring back more than 200 cigars, 800 cigarettes, 10 liters of spirits, and/or 90 liters of wine, you have to declare the goods upon return.

➤INFORMATION: HM Customs and Excise (Portcullis House, 21 Cowbridge Rd. E, Cardiff CF11 9SS, tel. 029/2038–6423 or 0845/010–9000, www.hmce.gov.uk).

## IN THE U.S.

U.S. residents who have been out of the country for at least 48 hours may bring home, for personal use, $800 worth of foreign goods duty-free, as long as they haven't used the $800 allowance or any part of it in the past 30 days. This exemption may include 1 liter of alcohol (for travelers 21 and older), 200 cigarettes, and 100 non-Cuban cigars. Family members from the same household who are traveling together may pool their $800 personal exemptions. For fewer than 48 hours, the duty-free allowance drops to $200, which may include 50 cigarettes, 10 non-Cuban cigars, and 150 milliliters of alcohol (or perfume containing alcohol). The $200 allowance cannot be combined with other individuals' exemptions, and if you exceed it, the full value of all the goods will be taxed. Antiques, which the U.S. Customs Service defines as objects more than 100 years old, enter duty-free, as do original works of art done entirely by hand, including paintings, drawings, and sculptures.

You may also send packages home duty-free, with a limit of one parcel per addressee per day (except alcohol or tobacco products or perfume worth more than $5). You can mail up to $200 worth of goods for personal use; label the package PERSONAL USE and attach a list of its contents and their retail value. If the package contains your used personal belongings, mark it PERSONAL GOODS RETURNED to avoid paying duties. You may send up to $100 worth of goods as a gift; mark the package UNSOLICITED GIFT. Mailed items do not affect your duty-free allowance on your return.

➤INFORMATION: U.S. Customs Service (for inquiries, 1300 Pennsylvania Ave. NW, Washington, DC 20229, www.customs.gov, tel. 202/354–1000; for complaints, Customer Satisfaction Unit, 1300 Pennsylvania Ave. NW, Room 5.5A, Washington, DC 20229; for registration of equipment, Office of Passenger Programs, 1300 Pennsylvania Ave. NW, Room 5.4D, Washington, DC 20229, tel. 202/927–0530).

# Disabilities and Accessibility

Ireland has only recently begun to provide facilities such as ramps and accessible toilets for people with disabilities. Public transportation also lags behind. However, visitors with disabilities will often find that the helpfulness of the Irish makes up for the lack of amenities.

➤**LOCAL RESOURCES: Disability Action** (2 Annadale Ave., Belfast, tel. 028/9029–7880, www.disabilityaction.org). **National Disability Resource Center** (44 N. Great George's St., Dublin, tel. 01/874–7503).

## LODGING

In the $$$$ category of hotels in Dublin, the Conrad Dublin International has some of the best amenities for people using wheelchairs. It has a ramped entrance, access to all floors, and bedrooms with adapted bathroom. For the $$$ range in Dublin, try the Doyle Burlington, though be warned that it has limited access and that many people using wheelchairs will need assistance in relation to the toilet facilities. In the $ category, offering the best services in any price range is Jurys Christchurch Inn or Jurys Customs House Inn. Both of these hotels are fully accessible to people using wheelchairs. In Belfast, the Belfast Hilton ($$$$) is fully accessible.

## RESERVATIONS

When discussing accessibility with an operator or reservations agent, **ask hard questions.** Are there any stairs, inside or out? Are there grab bars next to the toilet *and* in the shower/tub? How wide is the doorway to the room? To the bathroom? For the most extensive facilities meeting the latest legal specifications, **opt for newer accommodations.** If you reserve through a toll-free number, consider also calling the hotel's local number to confirm the information from the central reservations office. Get confirmation in writing when you can.

## TRANSPORTATION

Dublin airport is accessible for people using wheelchairs. Assistance will be needed at other airports.

The suburban rail system in Dublin (DART) is also accessible to most people using wheelchairs, but not all stations are accessible, so it is advisable to have some assistance present. The national rail system cars do not permit wheelchairs to move through the aisles, though accommodation can be made in the vestibule area of the carriage, which is spacious and air-conditioned. However, the passenger using a wheelchair will be isolated from fellow travelers.

People using wheelchairs will have difficulty on buses, as very few are equipped for wheelchairs; however, there are several taxi companies that operate wheelchair-accessible cars. Hand-controlled cars are no longer available for rent in Ireland due to the high cost of insurance.

Travelers with disabilities who display the wheelchair sign on their cars can park free of charge at parking meters in Dublin and in designated parking spaces. The Orange Badge issued to people with disabilities in the United Kingdom can be used while visiting Ireland.

➤COMPLAINTS: **Aviation Consumer Protection Division** (☞ Air Travel) for airline-related problems. **Departmental Office of Civil Rights** (for general inquiries, U.S. Department of Transportation, S-30, 400 7th St. SW, Room 10215, Washington, DC 20590, tel. 202/366–4648, fax 202/366–3571, www.dot. gov/ost/docr/index.htm). **Disability Rights Section** (NYAV, U.S. Department of Justice, Civil Rights Division, 950 Pennsylvania Ave. NW, Washington, DC 20530; tel. ADA information line 202/514–0301, 800/514–0301, 202/514–0383 TTY, 800/514–0383 TTY, www.usdoj.gov/crt/ada/adahom1.htm).

## TRAVEL AGENCIES

In the United States, the Americans with Disabilities Act requires that travel firms serve the needs of all travelers. Some agencies specialize in working with people with disabilities.

➤**TRAVELERS WITH MOBILITY PROBLEMS: Access Adventures** (206 Chestnut Ridge Rd., Scottsville, NY 14624, tel. 716/889–9096), run by a former physical-rehabilitation counselor. **CareVacations** (5-5110 50th Ave., Leduc, Alberta T9E 6V4, Canada, tel. 780/986–6404 or 877/478–7827, fax 780/986–8332, www.carevacations.com), for group tours and cruise vacations. **Flying Wheels Travel** (143 W. Bridge St., Box 382, Owatonna, MN 55060, tel. 507/451–5005, fax 507/451–1685, www.flyingwheelstravel.com).

➤**TRAVELERS WITH DEVELOPMENTAL DISABILITIES: New Directions** (5276 Hollister Ave., Suite 207, Santa Barbara, CA 93111, tel. 805/967–2841 or 888/967–2841, fax 805/964–7344, www.newdirectionstravel.com).

# Discounts and Deals

Tourists should take advantage of the Heritage Service Heritage Card. The card will give travelers access to 65 Heritage sites for €19.05 or €45.70 for a family pass. Cards are sold in Ireland at all Heritage Service sites.

Be a smart shopper and **compare all your options** before making decisions. A plane ticket bought with a promotional coupon from travel clubs, coupon books, and direct-mail offers may not be cheaper than the least expensive fare from a discount ticket agency. And always keep in mind that what you get is just as important as what you save.

## DISCOUNT RESERVATIONS

To save money, **look into discount reservations services** with toll-free numbers, which use their buying power to get a better price on hotels, airline tickets, even car rentals. When booking a room, always **call the hotel's local toll-free number** (if one is available) rather than the central reservations number—you'll often get a better price. Always ask about special packages or corporate rates.

When shopping for the best deal on hotels and car rentals, **look for guaranteed exchange rates**, which protect you against a falling dollar. With your rate locked in, you won't pay more, even if the price goes up in the local currency.

➤**AIRLINE TICKETS: tel. 800/AIR–4LESS.**

➤**HOTEL ROOMS: Hotel Reservations Network** (tel. 800/964–6835, www.hoteldiscount.com). **Players Express Vacations** (tel. 800/458–6161, www.playersexpress.com). **Steigenberger Reservation Service** (tel. 800/223–5652, www.srs-worldhotels.com). **Travel Interlink** (tel. 800/888–5898, www.travelinterlink.com). **Turbotrip.com** (tel. 800/473–7829, www.turbotrip.com).

## PACKAGE DEALS

Don't confuse packages and guided tours. When you buy a package, you travel on your own, just as though you had planned the trip yourself. Fly-drive packages, which combine airfare and car rental, are often a good deal. If you **buy a rail-drive pass,** you may save on train tickets and car rentals. All Eurail- and Europass holders get a discount on Eurostar fares through the Channel Tunnel.

# Embassies

Embassies are open weekdays 9–1 and 2–5.

➤**AUSTRALIA:** Fitzwilton House, Wilton Terr., South of the Liffey, tel. 01/676–1517.

➤**CANADA:** 65 St. Stephen's Green, South of the Liffey, tel. 01/478–1988.

➤**NEW ZEALAND:** New Zealand House, The Haymarket, London SW1Y 4TQ, tel. 44/20/7930-8422.

➤**SOUTH AFRICA:** Earlsfort Centre, South of the Liffey, tel. 01/661-5553.

➤**UNITED KINGDOM:** 29 Merrion Rd., South of the Liffey, tel. 01/205-3700.

➤**UNITED STATES:** 42 Elgin Rd., South of the Liffey, tel. 01/668-8777.

## Emergencies

Call Dublin's Eastern Help Board for the names of doctors. The Dublin Dental Hospital has emergency facilities and lists of dentists who offer emergency care. Hamilton Long, a Dublin pharmacy, is open Monday–Wednesday and Saturday 8:30–6, Thursday 8:30–8, and Friday 8:30–7. Temple Bar Pharmacy is open Monday–Wednesday and Friday–Saturday 9–7, Thursday 9–8.

➤**DOCTORS AND DENTISTS: Dublin Dental Hospital** (20 Lincoln Pl., South of the Liffey, tel. 01/662–0766). **Eastern Help Board** (tel. 01/679–0700).

➤**EMERGENCY SERVICES: Gardai (police), ambulance, fire** (tel. 999).

➤**HOSPITALS: Beaumont** (Beaumont Rd., North County Dublin, tel. 01/837–7755). **Mater** (Eccles St., North of the Liffey, tel. 01/830–1122). **St. James's** (1 James St., Dublin West, tel. 01/453–7941). **St. Vincent's** (Elm Park, South County Dublin, tel. 01/269–4533).

➤**LATE-NIGHT PHARMACIES: Hamilton Long** (5 Upper O'Connell St., North of the Liffey, tel. 01/874–8456). **Temple Bar Pharmacy** (20 E. Essex St., Temple Bar, tel. 01/670–9751).

# Guidebooks

Plan well and you won't be sorry. Guidebooks are excellent tools—and you can take them with you. You may want to check out color-photo-illustrated guides such as *Fodor's Exploring Ireland*, which is thorough on culture and history, and *Fodor's Escape to Ireland*, which highlights unique experiences. Pocket-size *Citypack Dublin* includes a foldout map. All are available at on-line retailers and bookstores everywhere.

# Language

Irish (also known as Gaelic)—a Celtic language related to Scots Gaelic, Breton, and Welsh—is the official national language. Though English is technically the second language of the country, it is, in fact, the everyday tongue of 95% of the population. Nowadays all Irish speakers are fluent in English.

# Lodging

## BED-AND-BREAKFASTS

For a small fee, the Irish Tourist Board, known as Bord Fáilte, will book accommodations anywhere in Ireland through a central reservations system. B&Bs can be booked at local visitor information offices when they are open; however, even these reservations will go through the central system.

➤CONTACT INFORMATION: Bord Fáilte (tel. 800/223–6470 in the U.S. and Canada; 800/039–7000 in the U.K.; 02/9299–6177 in Australia; 09/379–8720 in New Zealand; www.irelandvacations. com, www.ireland.travel.ie).

## HOSTELS

No matter what your age, you can save on lodging costs by staying at hostels. In some 4,500 locations in more than 70 countries around the world, Hostelling International (HI), the umbrella group for a number of national youth-hostel associations, offers single-sex, dorm-style beds and, at many hostels, rooms for couples and family accommodations. Membership in any HI national hostel association, open to travelers of all ages, allows you to stay in HI-affiliated hostels at member rates; one-year membership is about $25 for adults (C$35 for a two-year minimum membership in Canada, £13 in the U.K., A$52 in Australia, and NZ$40 in New Zealand); hostels run about $10–$30 per night. Members have priority if the hostel is full; they're also eligible for discounts around the world, even on rail and bus travel in some countries.

➤ORGANIZATIONS: **Hostelling International—American Youth Hostels** (733 15th St. NW, Suite 840, Washington, DC 20005, tel. 202/783–6161, fax 202/783–6171, www.hiayh.org). **Hostelling International—Canada** (400–205 Catherine St., Ottawa, Ontario K2P 1C3, tel. 613/237–7884 or 800/663–5777, fax 613/237–7868, www.hihostels.ca). **Youth Hostel Association of England and Wales** (Trevelyan House, Dimple Rd., Matlock, Derbyshire DE4 3YH, U.K., tel. 0870/870–8808, fax 0169/592–702, www.yha.org.uk). **Youth Hostel Association Australia** (10 Mallett St., Camperdown, NSW 2050, tel. 02/9565–1699, fax 02/9565–1325, www.yha.com.au). **Youth Hostels Association of New Zealand** (Level 3, 193 Cashel St., Box 436, Christchurch, tel. 03/379–9970, fax 03/365–4476, www.yha.org.nz).

## Money Matters

A modest hotel in Dublin costs about €127 a night for two; this figure can be reduced to under €90 by staying in a registered guest house or inn, and reduced to less than €45 by staying in a suburban B&B. Lunch, consisting of a good one-dish plate of bar food at a pub, costs around €7.60; a sandwich at the same pub, about €2.55. In Dublin's better restaurants, dinner will run around €25.40–€38.10 per person, excluding drinks and tip. Theater and entertainment are inexpensive—about €17.80 for a good seat, and double that for a big-name, pop-music concert.

Prices throughout this guide are given for adults. Substantially reduced fees are almost always available for children, students, and senior citizens. For information on taxes, *see* Taxes.

## ATMS
ATMs are found in all major towns. Most major banks are connected to CIRRUS or PLUS systems; there is a four-digit maximum for your PIN.

## CREDIT CARDS
Throughout this guide, the following abbreviations are used: **AE,** American Express; **DC,** Diners Club; **MC,** MasterCard; and **V,** Visa.

►**REPORTING LOST CARDS: American Express** (tel. 0353/ 1205–5111). **Diners Club** (tel. 0353/661–1800). **MasterCard** (tel. 1800/557378). **Visa** (tel. 1800/558002).

## CURRENCY
Euro notes come in denominations of €500, €200, €100, €50, €20, €10 and €5. The euro is divided into 100 cents, and coins are available as €2 and €1 and 50, 20, 10, 5, 2, and 1 cents. The euro can be used in 11 other European countries: Austria, Belgium, Finland, France, Germany, Greece, Italy, Luxembourg, the Netherlands, Portugal, and Spain.

## CURRENCY EXCHANGE
Dollars and British pounds are accepted only in large hotels and shops geared to tourists. Elsewhere you will be expected to use the euro.

At press time, the euro stood at around U.S.$.88, Canadian $1.43, U.K.£.61, Australian $1.72, and New Zealand $2.09; however, these rates will inevitably change both before and during 2003. Keep a sharp eye on the exchange rate.

For the most favorable rates, **change money through banks.** Although ATM transaction fees may be higher abroad than at home, ATM rates are excellent because they are based on wholesale rates offered only by major banks. You won't do as well at exchange booths in airports or rail and bus stations, in hotels, in restaurants, or in stores. To avoid lines at airport exchange booths, get a bit of local currency before you leave home.

►EXCHANGE SERVICES: International Currency Express (tel. 888/278–6628 orders). Thomas Cook Currency Services (tel. 800/287–7362 orders and retail locations, www.us. thomascook.com).

## Passports and Visas

When traveling internationally, **carry your passport** even if you don't need one (it's always the best form of I.D.) and **make two photocopies of the data page** (one for someone at home and another for you, carried separately from your passport). If you lose your passport, promptly call the nearest embassy or consulate and the local police.

### ENTERING IRELAND
All U.S., Canadian, Australian, and New Zealand citizens, even infants, need a valid passport to enter Ireland for stays of up to 90 days. Citizens of the United Kingdom, when traveling on flights departing from Great Britain, do not need a passport to enter Ireland. Passport requirements for Northern Ireland are the same as for the Republic.

## Senior-Citizen Travel

To qualify for age-related discounts, **mention your senior-citizen status up front** when booking hotel reservations (not when checking out) and before you're seated in restaurants (not when paying the bill). When renting a car, ask about promotional car-rental discounts, which can be cheaper than senior-citizen rates.

➤**EDUCATIONAL PROGRAMS: Elderhostel** (11 Ave. de Lafayette, Boston, MA 02111-1746, tel. 877/426–8056, fax 877/426–2166, www.elderhostel.org). **Interhostel** (University of New Hampshire, 6 Garrison Ave., Durham, NH 03824, tel. 603/862–1147 or 800/733–9753, fax 603/862–1113, www.learn.unh.edu).

## Sightseeing Tours

### BUS TOURS

Dublin Bus has three- and four-hour tours of the city center that include Trinity College, the Royal Hospital Kilmainham, and Phoenix Park. The one-hour City Tour, with hourly departures, allows you to hop on and off at any of the main sites. Tickets are available from the driver or Dublin Bus. There's also a continuous guided open-top bus tour (€10), run by Dublin Bus, which allows you to hop on and off the bus as often as you wish and visit some 15 sights along its route. The company also conducts a north-city coastal tour, going to Howth, and a south-city tour, traveling as far as Enniskerry.

Gray Line Tours runs city-center tours that cover the same sights as the Dublin Bus itineraries. Bus Éireann organizes day tours out of Busaras, the main bus station, to country destinations such as Glendalough.

➤**FEES AND SCHEDULES: Bus Éireann** (tel. 01/836–6111). **Dublin Bus** (tel. 01/873–4222). **Gray Line Tours** (tel. 01/670–8822).

### TRAIN AND CARRIAGE TOURS

Guided tours of Dublin using the DART system are organized by Views Unlimited. Horse-drawn carriage tours are available around Dublin and in Phoenix Park. For tours of the park, contact the Department of the Arts, Culture and the Gaeltacht. Carriages can be hired at the Grafton Street corner of St. Stephen's Green, without prior reservations.

➤**FEES AND SCHEDULES: Department of the Arts, Culture and the Gaeltacht** (tel. 01/661–3111). **Views Unlimited** (8 Prince of Wales Terr., South County Dublin Bray, tel. 01/286–0164 or 01/285–6121).

## PUB AND MUSICAL TOURS

Dublin Tourism (☞ Visitor Information) has a booklet to its self-guided "Rock 'n Stroll" Trail, which covers 16 sites with associations to such performers as Bob Geldof, Christy Moore, Sinéad O'Connor, and U2. Most of the sites are in the city center and Temple Bar. The Traditional Musical Pub Crawl begins at Oliver St. John Gogarty's and moves on to other famous Temple Bar pubs. Led by two professional musicians who perform songs and tell the story of Irish music, the tour is given May–October, daily at 7:30 PM; the cost is €9. The Comedy Coach is a nightly hop-on, hop-off tour of Dublin pubs, clubs, and restaurants. There is nonstop entertainment on the bus—musicians and comics keep everyone happy between pints. A ticket costs around €15.

Colm Quilligan arranges highly enjoyable evening walks of the literary pubs of Dublin, where "brain cells are replaced as quickly as they are drowned." The *Dublin Literary Pub Crawl* is a 122-page guide to those Dublin pubs with the greatest literary associations; it's widely available in Dublin bookstores.

➤**FEES AND SCHEDULES: Colm Quilligan** (tel. 01/454–0228). **Music and Comedy Coach** (tel. 01/280–1899). **Oliver St. John Gogarty's** (Fleet St., Temple Bar). **Traditional Musical Pub Crawl** (Discover Dublin, 20 Lower Stephens St., City Center, tel. 01/478–0191).

## WALKING TOURS

At the same time historical and hilarious, two well-know Dublin actors adopt a host of characters in HonestDublin's inventive two-hour walking tour of Dublin's major sites. A favorite scenario is the "drunken guide." The tours run from June to

September, Monday to Friday at 11 AM and weekends at 11 AM and 3 PM. Meet at the front gates of Dublin Castle. The cost is €10 and it's worth every cent. Historical Walking Tours of Dublin, run by Trinity College history graduate students, are excellent two-hour tour introductions to Dublin. The Bord Fáilte–approved tour assembles from May to September at the front gate of Trinity College, daily at 11 AM and 3 PM, with an extra tour on Saturday and Sunday at noon, October to April on Friday to Sunday at noon. It costs €9. A Georgian/Literary Walking Tour leaves from Bewley's Oriental Café June–September daily at 11; each tour lasts approximately two hours and costs €9. Trinity Tours organizes walks of the Trinity College campus on weekends from March 17 (St. Patrick's Day) through mid-May and from mid-May to September daily; the half-hour tour costs €7.60 and includes admission to the *Book of Kells*; tours start at the college's main gate. If you choose the Zozimus Experience you'll get an enjoyable walking tour of Dublin's medieval past, with a particular focus on the seedy, including great escapes, murders, and mythical happenings. Led by a guide in costume, tours are by arrangement only and run from the main gate of Dublin Castle from 6:45 PM; it costs €9 per person. (Prepare yourself for a surprise.)

►**FEES AND SCHEDULES: Georgian/Literary Walking Tour** (tel. 01/496–0641). **Historical Walking Tours of Dublin** (tel. 01/878 0227). **HonestDublin Walking Tours** (tel. 01/672–9971). **Trinity Tours** (tel. 01/608–2320). **Zozimus Experience** (tel. 01/661–8646).

## Taxes

### VALUE-ADDED TAX

When leaving the Irish Republic, U.S. and Canadian visitors get a refund of the value-added tax (VAT), which currently accounts for a hefty 20% of the purchase price of many goods and 12.5% of those that fall outside the luxury category. Apart from clothing, most items of interest to visitors, right down to ordinary toilet soap, are rated at 20%. Most crafts outlets and department stores operate a system called Cashback, which enables U.S. and Canadian visitors to collect VAT rebates in the currency of their choice at Dublin or Shannon Airport on departure. Otherwise, refunds can be claimed from individual stores after returning home. Forms for the refunds must be picked up at the time of purchase, and the form must be stamped by customs before leaving Ireland (including Northern Ireland). Most major stores deduct VAT at the time of sale if goods are to be shipped overseas; however, there is a shipping charge. VAT is not refundable on accommodation, car rental, meals, or any other form of personal services received on vacation.

When leaving Northern Ireland, U.S. and Canadian visitors can also get a refund of the 17.5% VAT by the over-the-counter and the direct-export methods. Most larger stores provide these services upon request and will handle the paperwork. For the over-the-counter method, you must spend more than U.K.£75 in one store. Ask the store for Form VAT 407 (you must have identification—passports are best), to be given to customs when you leave the country. The refund will be forwarded to you in about eight weeks (minus a small service charge) either in the form of a sterling check or as a credit to your charge card. The direct-export method, where the goods are shipped directly to your home, is more cumbersome. VAT Form 407/1/93 must be certified by customs, police, or a notary public when you get home and then sent back to the store, which will refund your money.

Global Refund is a VAT refund service that makes getting your money back hassle-free. The service is available Europe-wide at 130,000 affiliated stores. In participating stores, ask for the Global Refund refund form (called a Shopping Cheque). Have it stamped like any customs form by customs officials when you leave the European Union (be ready to show customs officials what you've bought). Then take the form to one of the more than 700 Global Refund counters—conveniently located at every major airport and border crossing—and your money will be refunded on the spot in the form of cash, check, or a refund to your credit-card account (minus a small percentage for processing).

➤VAT REFUNDS: Global Refund (99 Main St., Ste. 307, Nyack, NY 10960, tel. 800/566–9828, fax 845/348–1549, www. globalrefund.com).

## Taxis

Official licensed taxis, metered and designated by roof signs, do not cruise. You'll find taxi stands beside the central bus station, and at train stations, O'Connell Bridge, St. Stephen's Green, College Green, and near major hotels; the Dublin telephone directory has a complete list. The initial charge is €2.30 with an additional charge of about €2 a kilometer thereafter. The fare is displayed on a meter (make sure it's on). You may, instead, want to phone a taxi company and ask for a cab to meet you at your hotel, but this may cost up to €2.55 extra. Hackney cabs, which also operate in the city, have neither roof signs nor meters and will sometimes respond to hotels' requests for a cab. Negotiate the fare before your journey begins. Although the taxi fleet in Dublin is large, the cabs are nonstandard and some cars are neither spacious nor in pristine condition. Cab Charge has a reliable track record. Metro is one of the city's biggest but also the busiest. VIP Taxis usually has a car available for a longer trip.

➤TAXI COMPANIES: Cab Charge (tel. 01/677–2222). Metro (tel. 01/668–3333). VIP Taxis (tel. 01/478–3333).

## Telephones

Ireland's telephone system is up to the standards of the United Kingdom and the United States. Direct-dialing is common; local phone numbers have five to eight digits. You can make international calls from most phones, and some cell phones also work here, depending on the carrier.

**Do not make calls from your hotel room** unless it's absolutely necessary. Practically all hotels add 200% to 300% to the cost of a call.

### AREA AND COUNTRY CODES

The country code for Ireland is 353; for Northern Ireland, which is part of the United Kingdom telephone system, 44. The local area code for Northern Ireland is 028. However, when dialing Northern Ireland from the Republic you can simply dial 048 without using the U.K. country code. When dialing an Irish number from abroad, drop the initial o from the local area code. The country code is 1 for the United States and Canada, 61 for Australia, 64 for New Zealand, and 44 for the United Kingdom.

### DIRECTORY AND OPERATOR ASSISTANCE

If the operator has to connect your call, it will cost at least one-third more than direct dial.

►**DIRECTORY INFORMATION: Republic of Ireland** (tel. 11811 for directory inquiries in the Republic and Northern Ireland; 11818 for U.K. and international numbers; 114 for operator assistance with international calls; 10 for operator assistance for calls in Ireland, Northern Ireland, and the U.K.). **Northern Ireland and the U.K.** (tel. 192 for directory inquiries in Northern Ireland and the U.K.; 153 for international directory inquiries, which includes the Republic; 155 for the international operator; 100 for operator assistance for calls in the U.K. and Northern Ireland).

## INTERNATIONAL CALLS

International dialing codes can be found in all telephone directories. The international prefix from Ireland is oo. For calls to Great Britain, dial 0044 before the exchange code, and drop the initial zero of the local code. For the United States and Canada dial 001, for Australia 0061, and for New Zealand 0064.

## LOCAL CALLS

To make a local call just dial the number direct. Public phones take either coins (€.25 for a call) or cards, but not both. At coin phones just pick up the receiver and deposit the money before you dial the number. At card phones pick up the receiver, wait until the display tells you to insert the card, then dial. In the Republic, €.25 will buy you a three-minute local call; around €1 is needed for a three-minute long-distance call within the Republic. In Northern Ireland, a local call costs 10p.

## LONG-DISTANCE CALLS

To make a long-distance call, just dial the area code, then the number.

The local code for Northern Ireland is 028, unless you are dialing from the Republic. If you are dialing Northern Ireland from the Republic, dial 048 or 4428, followed by the eight-digit number.

## LONG-DISTANCE SERVICES

AT&T, MCI, and Sprint access codes make calling long distance relatively convenient, but you may find the local access number blocked in many hotel rooms. First ask the hotel operator to connect you. If the hotel operator balks, ask for an international operator, or dial the international operator yourself. One way to improve your odds of getting connected to your long-distance carrier is to travel with more than one company's calling card (a hotel may block Sprint, for example, but not MCI). If all else fails, call from a pay phone.

➤ACCESS CODES: AT&T Direct (tel. 1800/550000 from the Republic of Ireland; 0500/890011 from Northern Ireland). MCI

**WorldPhone** (tel. 1800/551001 from the Republic of Ireland; 0800/890222 from Northern Ireland using BT; 0500/890222 using C&W). **Sprint International Access** (tel. 1800/552001 from the Republic of Ireland; 0800/890877 from Northern Ireland using BT; 0500/890877 using C&W).

### PHONE CARDS

"Callcards" are sold in all post offices and at most newsagents. These come in denominations of 10, 20, and 50 units and range in price from about €2.55 for 10 calls to €20.30 for 100 calls. Card phones are now more popular than coin phones.

## Tipping

In some hotels and restaurants a service charge of around 10%—rising to 15% in a few plush spots—is added to the bill. If in doubt, ask whether service is included. In places where it is included, tipping is not necessary unless you have received particularly good service. But if there is no service charge, add a minimum of 10% to the total.

Tip taxi drivers about 10% of the fare displayed by the meter. Hackney cabs, who make the trip for a prearranged sum, do not expect tips. There are few porters and plenty of baggage trolleys at airports, so tipping is usually not an issue; if you use a porter, €.65 is the minimum. Tip hotel porters about €.65 per large suitcase. Hairdressers normally expect about €1.30. You don't tip in pubs, but for waiter service in a bar, a hotel lounge, or a Dublin lounge bar, leave about €.65. It is not customary to tip for concierge service.

## Tours and Packages

Because everything is prearranged on a prepackaged tour or independent vacation, you'll spend less time planning—and often get it all at a good price.

## BOOKING WITH AN AGENT

Travel agents are excellent resources. But it's a good idea to collect brochures from several agencies, as some agents' suggestions may be influenced by relationships with tour and package firms that reward them for volume sales. If you have a special interest, **find an agent with expertise in that area**; the American Society of Travel Agents (ASTA; ☞ Travel Agencies) has a database of specialists worldwide.

Make sure your travel agent knows the accommodations and other services of the place being recommended. Ask about the hotel's location, room size, beds, and whether it has a pool, room service, or programs for children, if you care about these. Has your agent been there in person or sent others whom you can contact?

Do some homework on your own, too: local tourism boards can provide information about lesser-known and small-niche operators, some of which may sell only direct.

## BUYER BEWARE

Each year consumers are stranded or lose their money when tour operators—even large ones with excellent reputations—go out of business. So **check out the operator.** Ask several travel agents about its reputation, and try to **book with a company that has a consumer-protection program.** (Look for information in the company's brochure.) In the United States, members of the National Tour Association and the United States Tour Operators Association are required to set aside funds to cover your payments and travel arrangements in the event that the company defaults. It's also a good idea to choose a company that participates in the American Society of Travel Agents' Tour Operator Program (TOP); ASTA will act as mediator in any disputes between you and your tour operator.

Remember that the more your package or tour includes the better you can predict the ultimate cost of your vacation. Make sure you know exactly what is covered, and **beware of hidden** costs. Are taxes, tips, and transfers included? Entertainment and excursions? These can add up.

►**TOUR-OPERATOR RECOMMENDATIONS: American Society of Travel Agents** (ASTA; 1101 King St., Suite 200, Alexandria, VA 22314, tel. 800/965–2782 24-hr hot line, fax 703/739–3268, www.astanet.com). **National Tour Association** (NTA; 546 E. Main St., Lexington, KY 40508, tel. 859/226–4444 or 800/682–8886, www.ntaonline.com). **United States Tour Operators Association** (USTOA; 342 Madison Ave., Suite 1522, New York, NY 10173, tel. 212/599–6599 or 800/468–7862, fax 212/599–6744, www.ustoa.com).

# Train Travel

Dublin has two main train stations. Connolly Station provides train services to and from the east coast, Belfast, the north, and northwest. Heuston Station is the place for trains to and from the south and west. Pearse Station is for Bray and connections via Dun Laoghaire to the Liverpool-Holyhead ferries. Contact the Irish Rail Travel Centre for information.

An electric railway system, the DART (Dublin Area Rapid Transit), connects Dublin with Howth to the north and Bray to the south on a fast, efficient line. There are 25 stations on the route, which is the best means of getting to seaside destinations, such as Howth, Blackrock, Dun Laoghaire, Dalkey, Killiney, and Bray. Train services run from Heuston Station to Kildare Town west of Dublin via Celbridge, Sallins, and Newbridge. From Connolly Station you can catch a train to more distant locations like Malahide, Maynooth, Skerries, and Drogheda to the north of Dublin and Wicklow and Arklow to the south.

## CUTTING COSTS

To save money, **look into rail passes.** But be aware that if you don't plan to cover many miles you may come out ahead by buying individual tickets.

➤**INFORMATION AND PASSES: CIE Tours International** (100 Hanover Ave., Box 501, Cedar Knolls, NJ 07927, tel. 800/243–8687, www.cietours.com). **DER Travel Services** (9501 W. Devon Ave., Rosemont, IL 60018, tel. 888/337–7350, fax 800/282–7474 or 847/692–4165, www.dertravel.com). **Rail Europe** (44 S Broadway, No. 11, White Plains, NY 10601, tel. 800/438–7245, fax 800/432–1329, www.raileurope.com; 2087 Dundas E, Suite 105, Mississauga, Ontario L4X 2V7, tel. 800/361–7245, fax 905/602–4198).

## FARES AND SCHEDULES

DART service starts at 6:30 AM and runs until 11:30 PM; at peak periods, 8–9:30 AM and 5–7 PM, trains arrive every five minutes. At other times of the day, the intervals between trains are 15 to 25 minutes. Call ahead to check precise departure times (they do vary, especially on bank holidays). Tickets can be bought at stations, but it's also possible to buy weekly rail tickets, as well as weekly or monthly "rail-and-bus" tickets, from the Irish Rail Travel Centre. Individual fares begin at €.85 and range up to €1.65. You'll pay a heavy penalty for traveling the DART without a ticket. For the Railways and DART Lost and Found, contact the Irish Rail Travel Centre.

➤**TRAIN INFORMATION: Connolly Station** (Amiens St., North of the Liffey). **DART** (tel. 01/836–6222). **Heuston Station** (end of Victoria Quay, Dublin West). **Irish Rail Travel Centre** (35 Lower Abbey St., North of the Liffey, tel. 01/836–6222). **Pearse Station** (Westland Row, South of the Liffey).

## Travel Agencies

A good travel agent puts your needs first. Look for an agency that has been in business at least five years, emphasizes customer service, and has someone on staff who specializes in your destination. In addition, **make sure the agency belongs to a professional trade organization.** The American Society of Travel Agents (ASTA)—the largest and most influential in the field, with more than 24,000 members in some 140 countries—maintains and enforces a strict code of ethics and will step in to help mediate any agent-client disputes if necessary. ASTA (whose motto is "without a travel agent, you're on your own") also maintains a Web site that includes a directory of agents. (If a travel agency is also acting as your tour operator, *see* Buyer Beware in Tours & Packages.)

➤**LOCAL AGENT REFERRALS: American Society of Travel Agents** (ASTA; 1101 King St., Suite 200, Alexandria, VA 22314, tel. 800/965–2782 24-hr hot line, fax 703/739–3268, www.astanet.com). **Association of British Travel Agents** (68–71 Newman St., London W1T 3AH, tel. 020/7637–2444, fax 020/7637–0713, www.abtanet.com). **Association of Canadian Travel Agents** (130 Albert St., Suite 1705, Ottawa, Ontario K1P 5G4, tel. 613/237–3657, fax 613/237–7052, www.acta.ca). **Australian Federation of Travel Agents** (Level 3, 309 Pitt St., Sydney, NSW 2000, tel. 02/9264–3299, fax 02/9264–1085, www.afta.com.au). **Travel Agents' Association of New Zealand** (Level 5, Tourism and Travel House, 79 Boulcott St., Box 1888, Wellington 6001, tel. 04/499–0104, fax 04/499–0827, www.taanz.org.nz).

➤**IN DUBLIN: American Express** (116 Grafton St., City Center, tel. 01/677–2874). **Thomas Cook** (118 Grafton St., City Center, tel. 01/677–1721).

## Visitor Information

➤**ITB: Ireland** (Baggot St. Bridge, Dublin 2, tel. 01/602–4000, 669/792083, or 1850/230330 [within Ireland], fax 01/602–4100). **U.K.** (Ireland House, 150 New Bond St., London W1Y 0AQ, tel. 020/7493–3201, fax 020/7493–9065). **U.S.** (345 Park Ave., New York, NY 10154, tel. 212/418–0800 or 800/223–6470, fax 212/371–9052).

➤**TOURIST INFORMATION: Bord Fáilte** (Baggot St. Bridge, South of the Liffey, tel. 01/602–4000; 1850/230330 [within Ireland], fax 01/602–4100, www.ireland.travel.ie). **Dublin Tourism** (Suffolk St., off Grafton St., City Center, tel. 01/605–7700; 1850/230330 [within Ireland], fax 01/605–7787, www.visitdublin.com). **Temple Bar Information Centre** (18 Eustace St., Temple Bar, tel. 01/671–5717, fax 01/677–2525).

## Web Sites

Do check out the World Wide Web when planning your trip. You'll find everything from weather forecasts to virtual tours of famous cities. Be sure to visit **Fodors.com** (www.fodors.com), a complete travel-planning site. You can research prices and book plane tickets, hotel rooms, rental cars, vacation packages, and more. In addition, you can post your pressing questions in the Travel Talk section. Other planning tools include a currency converter and weather reports, and there are loads of links to travel resources.

## When to Go

Summer remains the most popular time to visit Ireland, and for good reason. The weather is pleasant, the days are long (daylight lasts until after 10 in late June and July), and the countryside is green and beautiful. But there will be crowds in popular holiday spots, and prices for accommodations are at their peak. Unless you are determined to enjoy the short (July and August) swimming season, you would be well advised to take your vacation in Ireland outside peak travel months.

### CLIMATE

What follows are average daily maximum and minimum temperatures for Dublin.

➤**FORECASTS: Weather Channel Connection** (tel. 900/932–8437), 95¢ per minute from a Touch-Tone phone.

| | | | | | | | | |
|------|-----|-----|------|-----|-----|-------|-----|-----|
| Jan. | 47F | 8C | May | 59F | 15C | Sept. | 63F | 17C |
| | 34 | 1 | | 43 | 6 | | 49 | 9 |
| Feb. | 47F | 8C | June | 65F | 18C | Oct. | 58F | 14C |
| | 36 | 2 | | 49 | 9 | | 43 | 6 |
| Mar. | 50F | 10C | July | 68F | 20C | Nov. | 50F | 10C |
| | 38 | 3 | | 52 | 11 | | 40 | 4 |
| Apr. | 56F | 13C | Aug. | 67F | 20C | Dec. | 47F | 8C |
| | 40 | 4 | | 52 | 11 | | 38 | 3 |

# index

## ICONS AND SYMBOLS

★ Our special
recommendations
👍 Good for kids
(rubber duck)
③ ❸ Numbers in white
and black circles
that appear on the
maps, in the
margins, and
within the tours
correspond to one
another.

## A

A-Wear (department
store), 104
Abbey Presbyterian
Church, 61, 62
Abbey Tavern, 136
Abbey Theatre, 8, 126
Airport and environs
hotels, 158–159
Ambassador, 125
An Táin (shop), 111
Andrew's Lane Theatre,
126
Anna Livia statue, 69
Antiques and
collectibles, 106
Antiques fair, 106
Arbour Hill Cemetery, 74
Ardagh Chalice, 37
Ariel Guest House, 154
Ark, 41, 42
Arlington Hotel, 156

Arnotts (department
store), 104
Art galleries, 19, 25, 29–
30, 35, 35–36, 42–43, 55–56, 59,
66–67, 102–103, 122–124
Arthouse, 41, 42–43
Arts, 122–127
August Antiques Fair, 34
Avalon House, 146

## B

Bad Ass Café, 92
Ballsbridge
hotels, 149–151, 154
Irish cabaret, 136
restaurants, 94
Bambrick's (pub), 71–72
Bank of Ireland, 18, 19
Bank of Ireland Arts
Center, 19, 124
Bars, 26
Beaches, 113
Beaufield Mews, 95
Belgo, 91
Berkeley Court, 149
Bewleys at Newlands
Cross, 158
Bewley's Oriental Cafés,
9, 18, 22
Bicycling, 114
Black Church Print
Studio, 123
Blackrock (shopping
center), 103
Blanchardstown
(shopping center), 104

Blarney Woollen Mills
(shop), 108, 111
Book of Kells, 28
Book stores, 106–108
Books Upstairs (shop),
107
Bowling, 114–115
Boyle Monument, 57
Bray Leisure Bowl, 114–
115
Brazen Head (pub), 130
Brewery, 53
Bridge, 122
Brittas Lodge Riding
Stables, 116
Brown Thomas
(department store), 23,
104, 108
Browne's Brasserie, 83
Bruno's, 94
Burdock's, 88
Bushy Park, 117
Byrnes (pub), 129

## C

Cabaret, Irish, 136
Cassidy's (pub), 130
Castle Inn (pub), 136
Castle Vaults, 51
Castles, 51–52
Cathach Books (shop),
107
Cellar Bar (pub), 130–131
Celtic Note (music
store), 110
Cemeteries, 24, 74

Central Bank, 42, 43
Central Hotel, 146–147
Charleville Lodge, 156–157
Chapter One, 95–96
Chester Beatty Library, 46, 47
Chesterfield Avenue, 75
Chief O'Neill's Hotel, 131, 155
Children, attractions for,
Ark, 42
Chimney, 47
Dublinia, 46, 52
Phoenix Park, 75–76
zoo, 75–76
Chimney, 47
China, crystal, ceramics, and jewelry, 108–109
China Showrooms, 108
Christ Church Cathedral, 46, 50
Church of the Holy Trinity, 51–52
Church of St. Theresa's, 25
Churches, 25, 35, 39, 50, 51–52, 56–57, 59, 62, 69, 70
City Center
dance clubs, 137–138
Irish cabaret, 136
Northside hotels, 154–157
Northside restaurants, 95–97
pubs, 130–132, 134
shopping, 100, 102–103
sightseeing, 17–19, 22–30
Southside hotels, 142–147
Southside restaurants, 82–83, 86–91
City Hall, 46, 50–51
Claddagh Records, 110

Clarence, 147–148
Clarion Hotel IFSC, 155–156
Clarion Stephen's Hall Hotel & Suites, 145
Classical music, 124
Cleo Ltd. (shop), 111
Clery's (department store), 104
Clontarf Castle, 136
Cobblestone (pub), 9, 131
Collins Barracks, 38, 74
Comhaltas Ceoltóirí Éireann (dance club), 137
Commons Restaurant, 87
Conlon Antiques, 106
Connolly, James, 53, 65
Conrad Dublin International, 142–143
Contemporary music, 125–126
Conway's (pub), 69
Cooke's Café, 82
Cork Hill Gate, 52
County Dublin suburbs
Irish cabaret, 136
pubs, 135
shopping, 103–104
Crafts Centre of Ireland, 108
Crannóg (shop), 108
Credit cards, 179
Cross of Cong, 37
Curragh, 119
Custom House, 61, 62–63

D
Dancing and dance clubs, 137–138
Daniel O'Connell monument, 68
Davenport, 144–145

Davy Byrne's (pub), 97, 131
Dawson Street, 100
Deer Park, 115
Deerpark Riding Center, 116
Department stores, 104–105
Designyard (shop), 108
Diep Le Shaker, 90
Dining. ☞ See Pubs; Restaurants
Dish, 93
Dobbins, 87
Dockers (pub), 131
Doheny & Nesbitt (pub), 131
Donnybrook, 95
Douglas Hyde Gallery of Modern Art, 29–30
Doyle Burlington, 136, 150–151
Doyle's (pub), 131
Drury Court Hotel, 145–146
Dublin airport hotels, 158–159
Dublin Bookshop, 107
Dublin Castle, 46, 51–52
Dublin Civic Museum, 18, 22
Dublin Experience, 30
Dublin Tourism, 18, 23
Dublin Woollen Mills (shop), 111
Dublin Writers Museum, 8, 61, 63–64
Dublin Zoo, 75, 77
Dubliner Pub, 129
Dublinia, 46, 52
Dundrum Family Recreation Center, 117
Dunnes Stores (department store), 104

**E**

Eason's (department store), 105

Eason's/Hanna's (bookstore), 107

Easter Uprising, 38, 53, 64, 65

Eden, 92–93

Edmonstown, 115

Elephant & Castle, 91–92

Elm Park, 115

Emmett, Robert, 53

Ernie's Restaurant, 95

**F**

Fairyhouse, 119

5th (art gallery), 122

Film, 44, 124–125

Fitzer's, 36

Fitzpatrick Castle Dublin, 157–158

Fitzwilliam Hotel, 143

Flip (shop), 111

Flying Pig Bookshop, 107

Football, 118

Football Association of Ireland, 118

Forty Foot Bathing Pool, 117

Four Courts, 46, 52–53

Four Seasons, 149–150

Foxrock, 115

Francis Street, 100

Front Lounge (pub), 135

**G**

GAA Museum, 61, 64

Gael Linn (music store), 110

Gaelic Athletic Association (GAA), 118

Gaelic games, 118

Gaiety Theatre, 126

Gallery of Photography, 42, 43

Garden of Remembrance, 61, 64

Gardens, 24–25, 26–27, 64, 75

Gate Theatre, 61, 64–65, 70, 127

Gay and lesbian pubs, 117

Genealogical Office, 32

General Post Office (GPO), 61, 65

George (pub), 136

George's Street Arcade, 18, 23

Georgian Dublin, 31–39

Globe (pub), 131–132

Globetrotters Tourist Hotel, 157

Golf, 115–116

Golf D2, 115–116

Government Buildings, 31, 33

Grafton Street, 18, 23–24, 100

Grand Canal district, 70–73

Gravity Bar, 53

Great Courtyard, 51

Great Southern Hotel, 159

Green on Red Galleries, 122–123

Greene's (bookstore), 107

Gresham, 69

Greyhound racing, 119

Grogans (pub), 132

Gubu (pub), 136

Guinness Brewery and Storehouse, 46, 53

**H**

Halo, 96

Ha'penny Bridge, 41, 43

Ha'penny Bridge Galleries, 106

Harbor Master, 96

Harcourt Hotel, 137

Harolds Cross, 119

Health clubs, 116

Henry Street, 100

Heraldic Museum, 32

Herbert Park, 114, 117

Herbert Park Hotel, 150

Hermitage, 115

Hibernian Hotel, 151

HMV (music store), 110

Hodges Figgis (bookstore), 107

Hogan's (pub), 132

Holiday Inn Dublin Airport, 158–159

Homes, historic, 24–25, 33–34, 38–39, 67–68

Horse racing, 119

Horseback riding, 116

Horseshoe Bar, 26, 132

Hot Press Irish Music Hall of Fame, 61, 65–66

Hotels, 25–26, 141–142

City Center (Northside), 154–156

City Center (Southside), 142–147

Dublin Airport area, 158–159

price categories, 142

South City Center—Ballsbridge, 149–151, 154

South County Dublin Suburbs, 157–158

Temple Bar, 147–149

House of Ireland (shop), 109

House of Lords, 19

HQ, 125
HQ Gallery, 102–103
Hugh Lane Municipal Gallery of Modern Art, 61, 66–67
Hughes & Hughes (bookstores), 107
Huguenot Cemetery, 18, 24

**I**

Icons and symbols, 195
Il Primo, 88
Ilac Center (shopping center), 102
International Bar, 125
Irish cabaret, 136
Irish Film Centre (IFC), 41, 44, 124
Irish Film Centre Café, 44
Irish Jewish Museum, 71, 72
Irish Museum of Modern Art, 55–56
Irish music and dancing, 137
Irish Rugby Football Union, 119
Iveagh Fitness Club, 116
Iveagh Gardens, 24–25
Iveagh Market Hall, 58, 59

**J**

Jackie Skelly Fitness Centre, 116
Jaipur, 86
James Joyce Cultural Centre, 61, 67–68
Jazz music, 128
Jenny Vander (shop), 111
Jervis Shopping Centre, 102
JJ Smyth's (jazz club), 129

Jogging, 116–117
John Fallons (pub), 130
John M. Keating (pub), 69
Johnnie Fox's (pub), 135
Johnson's Court, 25
Joy of Coffee/Image Gallery Café, 45
Joyce, James, 26, 67–68
Joyce Museum, 68
Jurys Ballsbridge and the Towers, 129, 150
Jurys Christchurch Inn, 147
Jurys Hotel, 136
Jurys Skylon, 159
Jurys Tara, 158

**K**

Kavanagh, Patrick, 71, 72–73
Kehoe's (pub), 132
Kenilworth Bowling Club, 114
Kerlin Gallery, 123
Kevin and Howlin (shop), 111
Khyber Tandoori, 83, 86
Kiely's (pub), 130
Kilkenny Kitchen, 88
Kilkenny Shop, 109
Killiney, 113
Kilmainham Gaol, 46, 53–54
Kilronan House, 147
Kilternan Tennis Centre, 118
Kitchen (dance club), 138
Kitty O'Shea's (pub), 130

**L**

La Stampa, 82–83
Lansdowne Hotel, 154

Lansdowne Lawn Tennis Club, 118
Lansdowne Road Stadium, 118, 119
Le Méridien Shelbourne, 143
Leeson Street, 137
Leinster House, 31, 33–34
Leisureplex Coolock, 115
Lemon Crêpe and Coffee Co., 87
Leopardstown, 119
Les Frères Jacques, 93–94
Liberties district, 57–59
Liberty Market, 105
Libraries, 28–29, 30, 37, 39, 47, 54
Liffey River district, 59–70
Lillie's Bordello (dance club), 137
Locks, 83
Lodging. ☞ See Hotels
Long Hall Pub, 23
Lord Mayor's Lounge, 26

**M**

Malahide, 113
Mansion House, 32, 34
Mao, 90
Markets
covered market, 23, 59
outdoor, 105
Marks & Spencer (department store), 23, 105
Marsh's Library, 46, 54
McCullogh Piggott (music store), 110
McDaid's (pub), 132
McDonald's (bike shop), 114
McDowell (shop), 109
Meal plans, 142

Meeting House Square, 41, 44

Meeting House Square Market, 105

Mermaid Café, 93

Merrion Hotel, 143–144

Merrion Square, 31, 34–35

Metro Bowl, 115

Mike's Bike Shop, 114

Milano, 89

Modern Green Bar, 132

Monaghan's (shop), 111

Moore, Henry, 26

Moore Street, 105

Morrison Hotel, 154

Mother Redcap's Tavern (pub), 132

Mount Herbert Hotel, 151, 154

Mount Street Bridge, 71, 72

Mountjoy Square, 61, 68

Mulligan's, 132, 134

Museum stores, 36, 109

Museums, 23, 32, 37–38, 55–56, 63–64, 65–66, 67, 68

Music, 8–9, 124, 125–126 stores, 110

**N**

Nassau Street, 102

National College of Art and Design, 59

National Concert Hall, 124

National Gallery of Ireland, 32, 35–36, 67

National Gallery of Ireland Shop, 36, 109

National Library, 32, 37

National Museum, 32, 37–38

National Museum Annexe, 38

National Museum Shop, 108

National Photographic Archive, 123

Natural History Museum, 31, 38

Neary's (pub), 134

Nelson's Pillar, 68

New Berkeley Library, 30

New Project Arts Centre, 127

Newlands, 115

Newman House, 18, 24–25

Nightclubs, 137–138

Nightlife, 127–139

North Bull Island, 113

Northside City Center. ☞ See City Center

Nude, 91

Number 31, 146

Number Twenty-Nine, 31, 38–39

**O**

Obelisk, 75

O'Brien's (pub), 130

O'Carolan, Turlough, 57

O'Connell Bridge, 69

O'Connell, Daniel, 34–34, 68

O'Connell Street, 61–62, 68–69, 100

O'Connell's, 94

O'Donoghue's (pub), 134

Old Dublin, 91

Old Jameson Distillery, 46, 54–55

Old Library, 29

Old Stand (pub), 97, 134

Oliver St. John Gogarty (pub), 135

Olympia Theatre, 9, 42, 44–45, 125, 127

101 Talbot, 96–97

One Pico, 87–88

O'Neills (pub), 97

Opera, 124

Opera Ireland, 124

Opera Theatre Company, 124

Original Print Gallery, 123

Orwell Club, 116

Osteria Romano, 94

O'Sullivan Antiques, 106

Out on the Liffey (pub), 136

Outdoor activities and sports, 113–119

**P**

Palace Bar (pub), 135

Paramount Hotel, 148–149

Parks, 26–27, 75–76, 117

Parliament Hotel, 148

Parnell, Charles Stewart, 53

Pasta Fresca, 89

Patrick Guilbaud, 86

Patrick Kavanagh statue, 71, 72–73

Peacock Alley, 82

Peacock Theater, 126

Pearse, Pádrig, 53, 65

Pendulum Club, 129

People's Garden, 75

Phoenix Column, 75

Phoenix Park and environs, 73–76

Pod (dance club), 138

Point, 125–126

Porterhouse (pub), 135

Powerscourt Townhouse Centre (shopping center), 18, 25, 102–103

Price categories
dining, 81
lodging, 142
Pro-Cathedral, 61, 69
Pubs, 9–10, 23, 69, 71–72, 76, 97, 129–138
Punchestown, 119

**Q**

Quick tours, 10–13

**R**

Record Tower, 51
Red Box (dance club), 138
Renards (dance club), 138
Restaurants, 22, 36, 44, 69, 79–81. ☞ Also Pubs
American, 82
American casual, 91–92
Contemporary, 82–83, 92–93, 95–96
Continental, 83, 95
Ethnic, 83, 86
French, 86–87, 93–94
Irish, 87–88, 95
Italian, 88–89, 94
Japanese, 89–90
Mediterranean, 94, 96–97
Pan-Asian, 90
price categories, 81
Russian, 91
Vegetarian, 91
RHA Gallagher Gallery, 18, 25
RíRa (dance club), 138
Roches Stores, 105
Rock Music, 125–126
Rotunda Hospital, 61–62, 70
Round Drawing Room, 51
Royal Dublin Hotel, 156

Royal Hibernian Way (shopping center), 103
Royal Hospital Kilmainham, 46, 55–56, 124
Royal Irish Academy, 32, 39
Royal Marine Hotel, 157
Rubicon Gallery, 123
Rugby, 119
Ryan's Pub, 77, 134

**S**

St. Ann's Church, 32, 39
St. Anne's Park, 117–118
St. Francis Xavier Church, 61, 70
St. Michan's Church, 46, 56
St. Nicholas of Myra's Church, 58, 59
St. Patrick's Bell, 37
St. Patrick's Cathedral, 46, 56–57
St. Patrick's Hall, 51
St. Patrick's Well, 57
St. Stephen's Church, 35, 124
St. Stephen's Green, 18, 26–27
St. Stephen's Green Centre (shopping center), 103
St. Vincent's, 117
Samuel Beckett Centre, 127
Sandymount Strand, 113
Savoy Cinema, 125
Screen Cinema, 125
Scruffy Murphy's (pub), 71, 72
Shanahan's, 82
Shaw, George Bernard birthplace, 32, 39
Shelbourne Bar, 26

Shelbourne Méridien Hotel, 18, 25–26, 143
Shelbourne Park, 119
Shopping
antiques, 106
books, 106–108
centers, 102–104
china, crystal, ceramics, and jewelry, 108–109
department stores, 104–1
markets, 23, 59, 105
museum stores, 36, 109
music, 110
streets, 98
sweaters and tweeds, 110–111
vintage clothing, 111
Soccer, 118
Solomon Gallery, 123
Soup Dragon, 88
South City Center
hotels, 149–151, 154
Irish cabaret, 136
pubs, 129–130, 136
restaurants, 94–95
South County Dublin Suburbs
hotels, 157–158
pubs, 135
South Dublin dance clubs, 137
Sports
participant, 114–118
spectator, 118–119
Stag's Head (pub), 97, 134
State Apartments, 51
Steps of Rome, 89
Stillorgan, 95
Stillorgan Bowl, 115
Superdome, 115
Sutton, 115
Sweaters and tweeds, 110–111

Swift's tomb, 57
Swimming, 117
Symbols and icons, 195

**T**

Tara Brooch, 37
Tea Room, 92
Temple Bar area
 dance clubs, 138
 hotels, 147–149
 pubs, 135
 restaurants, 91–94
 shopping, 102
 sightseeing, 32–45
Temple Bar Gallery, 123–124
Temple Bar Hotel, 148
Temple Bar Music Centre, 9, 126
Tennis, 117–118
Tennis Ireland, 118
Terenure College, 117
Theater, 44–45, 64–65, 70, 126–127
Thornton's, 86
Tierneys (shop), 109
Tivoli, 127
Toner's (pub), 134

Tower Design Centre (shopping center), 103
Tower Records (music store), 110
Townsend Street, 117
Tracks Cycles, 114
Trinity College, 8, 18, 26–30
Trinity College Library, 28
Trinity College Library Shop, 109
Turlough O'Carolan monument, 57

**U**

UGC Multiplex, 125
Ulysses (Joyce), 72

**V**

Vintage clothing, 110
Viper Room (dance club), 138
Virgin Megastore (music store), 110

**W**

Wagamama, 90
Waterstone's (bookstore), 107

Waterways Visitors Centre, 71, 73
Web sites, 193
Wedgwood Room, 51
Weir & Sons (shop), 109
Wellington, Duke of, 75
West Wood Lawn Tennis Club, 118
Westburn Mall, 103
Westbury Hotel, 144
Western Dublin, 45–47, 50–57
Westin Dublin, 145
Whelan's, 126
Whiskey distillery, 54–55
White Cross, 75
Williams Park, 117
Winding Stair (bookstore), 108
Woodbrook, 115

**Y**

Yamamori, 89–90
Yeats, William Butler, 26

**Z**

Zanzibar (pub), 97
Zoo, 75, 77

202

## FODOR'S POCKET DUBLIN

**EDITORS:** Nuha Ansari, Diane Mehta, Tom Mercer

**Editorial Contributors:** Graham Bolger, Anto Howard, Elizabeth A. Whisler

**Editorial Production:** Ira-Neil Dittersdorf

**Maps:** David Lindroth, *cartographer*; Bob Blake and Rebecca Baer, *map editors*

**Design:** Fabrizio La Rocca, *creative director*; Tigist Getachew, *art director*; Jolie Novak, *senior picture editor*; Melanie Marin, *photo editor*

**Production/Manufacturing:** Angela L. McLean

**Cover Photo** (Merrion Square): Abbie Enock; Travel Ink/Corbis

Fifth Edition

ISBN 1–4000–1110–8

ISSN 1098–965X

## IMPORTANT TIP

Although all prices, opening times, and other details in this book are based on information supplied to us at press time, changes occur all the time in the travel world, and Fodor's cannot accept responsibility for facts that become outdated or for inadvertent errors or omissions. So **ALWAYS CONFIRM INFORMATION WHEN IT MATTERS,** especially if you're making a detour to visit a specific place.

## SPECIAL SALES

Fodor's Travel Publications are available at special discounts for bulk purchases for sales promotions or premiums. Special editions, including personalized covers, excerpts of existing guides, and corporate imprints, can be created in large quantities for special needs. For more information, contact your local bookseller or write to Special Markets, Fodor's Travel Publications, 1745 Broadway, New York, NY 10019. Inquiries from Canada should be directed to your local Canadian bookseller or sent to Random House of Canada, Ltd., Marketing Department, 2775 Matheson Boulevard East, Mississauga, Ontario L4W 4P7. Inquiries from the United Kingdom should be sent to Fodor's Travel Publications, 20 Vauxhall Bridge Road, London SW1V 2SA, England.

PRINTED IN THE UNITED STATES OF AMERICA

10 9 8 7 6 5 4 3 2 1